# AMAZING SUN FUN ACTIVITIES

MICHAEL J. DALEY

ILLUSTRATED BY BUCKLEY SMITH

LEARNING
TRIANGLE
PRESS

*Connecting
kids, parents, and teachers
through learning*

**An imprint of McGraw-Hill**
New York  San Francisco  Washington, D.C.  Auckland
Bogotá  Caracas  Lisbon  London  Madrid  Mexico City
Milan  Montreal  New Delhi  San Juan
Singapore  Sydney  Tokyo  Toronto

## DEDICATION

For Cornelia Iselin—who inspired me

*McGraw-Hill*

*A Division of The **McGraw·Hill** Companies*

©1998 by **The McGraw-Hill Companies, Inc.**
Published by Learning Triangle Press, an imprint of McGraw-Hill.

Printed in the United States of America. All rights reserved.
The publisher takes no responsibility for the use of any materials or methods described in this book, nor for the products thereof.

pbk    1 2 3 4 5 6 7 8 9 MAL/MAL 9 0 2 1 0 9 8 7

ISBN 0-07-015177-6

Product or brand names used in this book may be trade names or trademarks. Where we believe that there may be proprietary claims to such trade names or trademarks, the name has been used with an initial capital or it has been capitalized in the style used by the name claimant. Regardless of the capitalization used, all such names have been used in an editorial manner without any intent to convey endorsement of or other affiliation with the name claimant. Neither the author nor the publisher intends to express any judgment as to the validity or legal status of any such proprietary claims.

**Library of Congress Cataloging-in-Publication Data applied for**

McGraw-Hill books are available at special quantity discounts. For more information, please write to the Director of Special Sales, McGraw-Hill, 11 West 19th Street, New York, NY 10011. Or contact your local bookstore.

Acquisitions editor: Judith Terrill-Breuer

Manuscript editor: Ellen James

Production supervisor: Claire B. Stanley

DTP production team: Computer artist supervisors: Nora Ananos, Tess Raynor
Computer artists: Charles Burkhour, Charles Nappa
Page makeup supervisor: Pat Caruso
Page makeup: Jaclyn J. Boone, Tanya Howden, Joanne Morbit

Designer: Jaclyn J. Boone                                                             DLY

# CONTENTS

# YOUR SOLAR LABORATORY

Hundreds of years of experience and careful thinking have taught people how to work with the sun. In this book you'll find out how solar energy is used in houses and to power machines. You will discover how much sunshine you eat every day, and how to build a solar hot water heater, cook solar S'mores, and bake mini-pizzas or tacos in a Pizza Box Solar Oven you build yourself. These and many more projects will let you put the sun to work right away!

Your solar laboratory is all outdoors. The sun shines in the windows of your house or apartment, in your back yard, in the city park, on the beach, in the school yard, on mountainsides, on rooftops, and even underwater. So you can do solar experiments just about anywhere you live, or play, or go to school.

Solar energy is a clean, renewable fuel. Most of the other fuels we use today, like oil and coal, are running out. They also cause dangerous pollution. Yet these fuels power most of our factories, heat our homes, run machines and computers. They power our cars, trucks, trains, and airplanes. Today, just as in the Rome of long ago, we are turning to solar energy to replace these fuels. There's a lot solar energy can already do. There's much more to be discovered. Maybe you will make some of those discoveries!

## SUN FACT

Enough sunshine falls on a 3' x 3' square to cook 18 hamburgers every hour. This amount of sunshine could also brew 40 cups of coffee, or fry 100 eggs!

## SUN FACT

In just one second, the sun makes enough energy to supply all the power people will need for the next 2,000 years.

## Turn fast food containers into hot projects

All tinkerers and inventors know this secret: The stuff many people throw away can be just the thing you need for your next experiment. Here's a list of things to collect for your solar junk box—so you can keep on hand the kind of junk that's good for building the solar projects in this book. If you like pizza, soda, and McDonald's, you won't have much trouble finding what you need. (Half the fun is eating what comes in the container first!)

## SUN FACT

Once you start saving things for your junk box, you won't have trouble believing that every family in the U.S. creates about 100 pounds of garbage every week! Altogether, people in the U.S. turn 3 million tons of food, paper, plastic, glass, metal, wood, and minerals into trash every week. This can't go on for very long before the Earth runs out of resources or chokes in pollution.

## Save:

- ❏ soda drink cups, tops, and straws
  (rinse them and let dry)

- ❏ pizza boxes

- ❏ shiny foil snack packages
  (chips, popcorn, etc.)

  *Be careful not to tear these when
  you open them up. You'll want
  to save a few really big bags
  and several smaller-sized ones.*

- ❏ plastic deli containers
  (wash in hot, soapy water and dry)

  *Many fast food restaurant salads
  come in these (McDonald's, Wendy's)
  as well as other kinds of ready-made
  deli foods. Try to find some with
  black bottoms and clear tops.*

- ❏ Dunkin' Donut boxes
  (Kentucky Fried Chicken, too)

- ❏ the paper bags take-out foods come in

- ❏ little white coffee creamer containers

- ❏ bubble pack

- ❏ quisp (styrofoam packing peanuts)

- ❏ empty soda can (rinsed out)

- ❏ big cardboard boxes of many sizes

## SUN FACT

Americans use over 66 billion
aluminum cans a year. If connected
end-to-end, they would make a chain
that could circle the sun—TWICE!
That's over six million miles long!

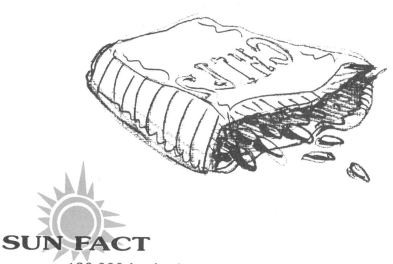

## SUN FACT

There are over 130,000 fast food
restaurants in the U.S.

VIII

## SUN FACT

Solar comes from the Latin word **solaris**, meaning sun.

# Cautions and hints for solar scientists

**NEVER LOOK DIRECTLY AT THE SUN, even with sunglasses on!**
The sun is so bright it can blind you.

**USE SHADOWS TO FIND THE SUN.**
When you need to aim an experiment at the sun, just look at its shadow. Turn your experiment until the shadow falls straight behind it. The aim will be perfect and you won't even have to peek at the sun.

**WEAR SUNGLASSES.** Sunglasses keep reflections out of your eyes. They make it easier to see when you work in bright sunlight.

**SLATHER ON THE SUNSCREEN.**
The rays of the sun are very powerful. They can heat water—or burn your skin if you stand in the sun too long. To protect your skin, use a sunscreen lotion (with ultraviolet —UV—protection) on all the bare places exposed to the sun.

## SUN FACT

In the United States, there are over 100,000 homes with solar electricity. Over 1.5 million families take baths in solar-heated water, and 300,000 families live in houses heated by the sun.

**HOT!!** Most temperatures in these experiments won't burn you. But always be safe. Before you pick up things heated with the sun, test how hot they are with a quick touch of your finger. Too hot? Use pot holders or towels.

**THERMOMETERS** are helpful if you want to know how well your solar experiments are working. Try to find a mercury-type thermometer that reads between 50° and 150° Fahrenheit. A candy thermometer can work well, but be careful—they're fragile!

**THE BEST TIME** to experiment is between 10 AM and 3 PM. Of course, the best time of year is summer and the warmer days of spring and fall. Clear skies mean more sunshine and the best chance for successful experiments.

**FOR BEST RESULTS**, when paint and plastic are called for, try to use a **flat black paint** (nontoxic, water-based latex), and **clear** plastic (like Saran-wrap).

# 1

# WHAT IS SOLAR ENERGY?

**HAVE YOU EVER . . . ?**

. . . wondered how the sun makes light and heat? Maybe not. Most people tend to take the sun for granted. After all, it has been there in the sky practically forever.

## SUN FACT

If you could drive a car 93 million miles from the Earth to the sun, it would take 150 years to get there. Because light travels much faster (180,000 miles per second), it takes only 8 minutes for the sun's light to reach the Earth.

The sun is the star at the center of our solar system and the source of solar energy. Solar energy is sent to Earth in invisible rays by the light and heat of the sun.

Before this century, many of the greatest scientists thought the sun might be a sort of bonfire in space, made of coal or wood. These scientists were making guesses about the sun. Since they knew the sun was 864,000 miles through the middle, they decided that a lump of coal that big could burn for about 5,000 years.

But then scientists learned that the Earth was over four billion years old, and that dinosaurs were running around over 200 million years ago. The sun could not be made of coal. Then new discoveries revealed that the sun was actually made of hydrogen and helium, elements which are gases on Earth.

## SUN FACT

The very first time scientists got a look at the sun from space was in the 1950s, when the first satellites were put into orbit by rockets.

# In the heart of the sun

The sun is actually more like a glowing electric stove burner. When you boil water, the electricity passing through the coils and causes them to glow red hot, but there's no fire. Deep inside the sun, radiation causes the gases that surround the center of the sun to get super hot. These gases give off heat and light without really burning. The radiation in the core of the sun comes from fusion. (To find out more about fusion, check out the "sun fact" below.)

The energy from the sun's core takes 50 million years to reach the surface, where it becomes light and travels into space. The sunshine you feel on your face today was created millions of years before people ever walked on the Earth!

## SUN FACT

The Nobel Prize–winning scientist, Hans Bethe, first figured out in 1938 how energy was created by the sun. The core of the sun is tremendously hot—27 million degrees Fahrenheit. Hydrogen atoms bump into each other constantly, like people trying to get into a subway train at rush hour. Some of these atoms stick together in pairs, creating helium. Each time the atoms stick together, they release energy in the form of radiation. So many atoms are fusing that it's like 100 billion hydrogen bombs exploding every second!

## SUN FACT

Solar wind is created when the sun sends high-energy
particles into space. As the solar wind blows by the Earth,
it causes huge, beautiful sheets of light to dance in the polar sky.
These displays are called the *aurora borealis*, or northern lights.
(They happen at the South Pole, too.)

## SUN FACT

Five million tons of the sun's mass
changes into energy **every second**,
yet the sun will keep on shining
for billions of years to come.

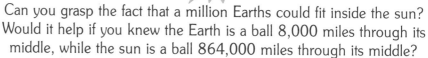

## SUN FACT

Can you grasp the fact that a million Earths could fit inside the sun?
Would it help if you knew the Earth is a ball 8,000 miles through its
middle, while the sun is a ball 864,000 miles through its middle?

## SUN FACT

Solar flares are geysers of sunlight
that erupt from the surface of the sun.
There is enough energy in one solar flare
to power all our cars, machines, houses,
and factories for one billion years!

# Make a model Earth & sun

Models help us understand things in the real world that are too big or too small for our eyes, hands, and minds to grasp. The real sun and Earth are so huge, it's almost impossible to imagine them. But what if the sun were only as big as a family-size pizza? Then the Earth would be about the size of a plain m&m®. Now we can get some perspective on things—like how far apart they are in space.

*What if the sun were as big as a family-size pizza?*

Get a cardboard pizza circle from a family-size pizza (or cut your own two-foot-wide circle from a cardboard box). Pretend this is the sun. Use a blue m&m® as a model of the Earth.

*Two-Foot-Wide*
*Pizza Circle*

*m & m*

Now take your model to a football field with two friends. Have one person hold up the sun at the goal line. Have another hold up the Earth at the 75-yard line. You can go up in the bleachers or stand on the sideline. This is what the sun and Earth might look like from far out in space. (Remember, the sun is 93 million miles from the Earth.)

You may even need binoculars to see the Earth!

## SUN FACT

Models are made to scale. The scale of a model tells you how much larger the real thing is than the model. The scale of this sun model is 36,000 to one. That means every inch on the model equals 36,000 miles on the real sun, which is 864,000 miles across the middle!

# The Earth's power plant

Without solar energy, the Earth would be dark, frozen, and empty. Although the sun warms all the planets, many scientists don't think there is currently life on any other planet in our solar system. What makes Earth special?

*The temperature of the Earth is just right for lizards!*

The Earth's atmosphere is the sun's partner. The air traps the heat of the sun. This makes the temperature of the Earth just right for plants, animals, bugs, people . . . and lizards!

It's not always perfectly comfortable on Earth. There are really cold places, and really hot places, and storms and tornadoes. Think of what it's like when you have lots of energy—you want to **do** something: run, jump, shout, play games. It's the same with all the solar energy the sun pours into the Earth every day. Things get stirred up.

## SUN FACT

Some of the sun's energy is dangerous radiation. A part of Earth's atmosphere, called the ozone layer, blocks out this harmful energy. Certain polluting chemicals open holes in the **ozone layer**, allowing more of the dangerous rays onto the Earth, hurting plants, animals, and people. This is why you have to wear sunscreen.

6

The sun doesn't warm the Earth evenly. The poles get little sunshine, and one whole side of the Earth is dark half the day. The warm air and cold air don't sit still. The warm air rises into the sky. The cold air sinks to the ground. At the same time, the Earth is whirling around on its axis, mixing up the moving air. All this commotion creates the wind.

Imagine a parking lot, soaking wet after a rain. What happens when the sun comes out? Where does the water go? The heat of the sun causes it to evaporate. Up in the sky, it forms into clouds. The clouds drift around with the wind. Eventually, the cloud will rain down to Earth again— maybe hundreds of miles away!

# You are solar-powered!

## DID YOU KNOW . . . ?

. . . that leaves are solar-powered food factories?
But unlike most factories, leaves are quiet.
You won't hear any machinery clanking
away if you stand next to a tree.
And here's another difference:
instead of pollution, leaves
produce oxygen—just what
you need to breathe!!

All plants have a substance in their leaves called
chlorophyll, a chemical that captures solar energy.
The captured solar energy lets the leaves turn
water and carbon dioxide from the air into food
for the plant.

Light from the sun gives plants the energy they
need to grow. The plants give *you* the oxygen
you need to breathe. But the cells of your skin
cannot use solar energy to make food.
People and animals have to eat plants.

8

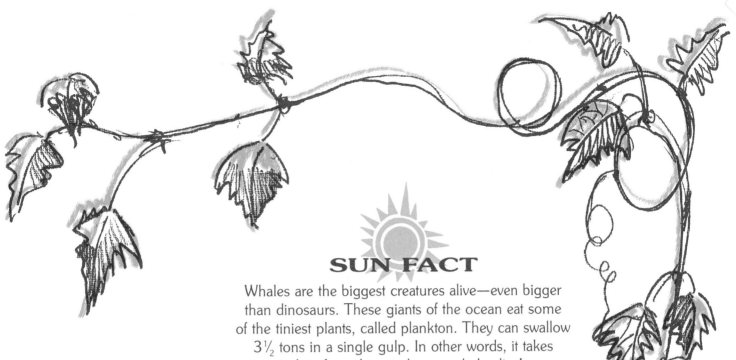

## SUN FACT

Whales are the biggest creatures alive—even bigger than dinosaurs. These giants of the ocean eat some of the tiniest plants, called plankton. They can swallow 3½ tons in a single gulp. In other words, it takes a lot of sunshine to keep a whale alive!

## SUN FUN

# How much sunshine do you eat?

Plants take time to grow from a tiny seed. Each day the plant grows by changing solar energy into food and storing it up in its leaves, seeds, or fruit. Let's say that one day of sunshine equals one stored-up sun day of energy. When you eat a plant (like a tomato), your body uses those stored-up sun days to keep alive.

Write down your favorite:

- vegetable _____    sun days _____

- fruit _____    sun days _____

- cereal _____    sun days _____

To find out the sun days for each, go to a garden store and look at seed packets. Some tomatoes, for example, take 90 days to grow. Or ask a farmer. Maybe your family grows a garden and you will already know the answer.

You won't find cereal seeds. You need to know what kind of grain your cereal is made from and find out the sun days for that.

Were you surprised by how much sunshine you eat?

# Science Fair Idea

Want to amaze people and maybe earn a gold star at the next science fair? Then find out how much solar energy you run on each day.

Keep track of all the food you eat in one day. Then trace each food to its original source in the plant world. Keep things simple—just pick the main ingredient. For instance, the main thing in a candy bar is sugar. Sugar comes from sugar cane. How many sun days are stored up in sugar cane?

This activity is a big challenge because you don't eat just vegetables. You might have a glass of milk, or a hamburger. Milk comes from cows. What plant does the cow eat to stay alive and make milk? How long does it take to grow? How long does a cow live before it is killed for hamburgers? How many sun days does a cow eat during those many months? You may want to talk to a biologist to find out!

Make a chart listing each food, the main ingredient, its source in the plant world, and the sun days. Add up all the sun days to get a grand total. Go for a double gold: include pictures of the foods and their plant sources!

# 2
# SUNSHINE DOESN'T STINK

## HAVE YOU EVER...?

. . . stood behind your school bus as
    it roared away from the curb?
    Pretty nasty, right?

That's pollution. If your school bus were powered with solar electricity,
you wouldn't be left standing in a black, stinky cloud. Most of the fuels we
use cause pollution. When coal is burned in factories, it makes dirty
smoke. Oil is black and gooey. When it is shipped in huge oil tankers, it
sometimes spills out, contaminating the ocean. Nuclear energy is used to
make electricity. But it also makes dangerous radioactive waste.

Fuels are sources of energy. Energy is absolutely necessary to modern life.
Energy keeps the lights on. It heats your house. It keeps your food cold, or
makes it hot with a quick zap in the microwave. Computers need energy. So
do televisions. When solar energy is used to heat a house, or warm up bath
water, or make electricity, it does not pollute. Nothing is burned up. There is
no smoke.

11

## SUN FACT

The sun has been shining for 5 billion years.
Scientists believe it will shine for another 5 billion years.
On the other hand, some experts predict that people will
probably run out of oil in 60 years.

## SUN FACT

Oil is sometimes called "dead dinosaurs"
because it is formed from the decayed
bodies of ancient animals and plants.
These animals and plants got their energy from
the sun. So oil is really million-year-old sunshine.

Solar energy is a very different fuel from oil or coal.
Solar energy is a clean fuel.

## The Earth is a piggy bank

Sunshine, wind power, and water power are all forms of renewable energy. No matter how much solar energy we use on Earth in any day, the sun will still be shining tomorrow. The wind caught in our windmill will be back again another day. The water that flows down the mountain will be lifted high into the sky by solar heat. It will rain down on the mountaintop once again.

Fuels like oil, coal, and gasoline are not renewable. Put a gallon of gas in the tank, take a trip, and where does the gas go? Right out the tailpipe as exhaust. If you put a huge balloon over the tailpipe and catch all the exhaust, can it be turned into gasoline again? Nope— when you use it, you lose it. Oil and coal are very valuable fuels, deposited deep within the Earth millions of years ago. There is only a limited amount of each—and, like having money in your piggy bank, the more you take out, the less there is.

## Your solar allowance

The energy that comes from the sun is more like an allowance. You can't spend more than you are given each day, but the same amount will be there day after day. Learning to live within our solar allowance means that people will have enough energy forever. Factories, homes, businesses, and transportation will run without causing pollution.

A fuel like wood is renewable. Trees are a kind of solar storage battery, turning solar energy into wood as they grow. But this is long, slow work. It takes a tree 20 or 30 years to grow from a seedling into a huge tree. When we use wood for fuel, we must always plant new trees to replace the ones we use.

## SUN FACT

Since 1776, people in the United States have cut down over 30 billion trees. Kids in Canton, Ohio, have planted more than 800,000 new trees as part of the America Free Tree Program. Their goal is one billion new trees by the year 2000. Want to help them? Contact your state forestry agent to find out about tree planting programs near you.

## SUN FUN

# Which ones are renewable?

Match each energy source on the left with the kind of work it might do. Connect your match with a line.

water power          runs engines
                     in cars

diesel fuel          makes the flame
                     for kitchen stoves

hay and oats         turns turbines at
                     hydroelectric dams

gasoline             feeds work horses
                     on farms

wind power           powers truck and
                     bus engines

propane gas          spins propellors
                     to make electricity

Answers:

water power — runs engines in cars
diesel fuel — powers truck and bus engines
hay and oats — feeds work horses on farms
gasoline — makes the flame for kitchen stoves
wind power — spins propellors to make electricity
propane gas — turns turbines at hydroelectric dams

Circle the energy sources you think are renewable. Which of these are always available, like solar energy? Which ones can people make renewable—like wood? Which energy sources will eventually run out?

15

## SUN FACT

Almost all the non-renewable fuels we use today come from beneath the Earth. Oil, coal, and natural gas are found far beneath the Earth's surface. Uranium has to be mined. But if you want fuel from the sun—just look up!

## SUN FACT

We are already using more renewable energy than nuclear power. The United States has so much sun, wind, water, and wood that some scientists think all our energy could come from renewable energy. How many of these energy sources can be found near you?

## SUN FUN
### Find south

To catch solar energy, people or objects have to be facing the sun, which comes from only one direction. In the Northern Hemisphere, where the United States is located, that direction is south. You will practice two methods to find south, even if the sun isn't shining. To try both ways, you will need a compass and a stick.

## Using the compass

Set the compass on a level surface. Watch the needle. When it stops moving, turn the compass slowly so the arrow tip lines up with the letter **N**, for north. South is opposite of north. East is where the sun comes up. West is where it sets.

## Using the stick

With a stick (and with less accuracy), you can find south only on a sunny day. Push the stick into the ground. At noon, the shadow will point roughly north. The opposite direction is south. It might be interesting to compare the shadow method with the compass. Is there a big difference?

# SUN FUN

## Follow the Leader

Plants can't walk around, but they do follow the sun as it moves across the sky. In the morning, carefully observe a houseplant, or a flower in a field. Which way is it facing? In the afternoon, look again. Have the leaves or the flowers moved?

# JOURNEY TO THE ANCIENT WORLD

## HAVE YOU EVER . . . ?

. . . measured your shadow at noontime and found it shorter in the summer than in the winter?

. . . noticed, as the months pass by, that the sun rises at a different place in the east and sets at a different place in the west?

**SUN FACT**

**How did they do it?**

More than 4,000 years ago, prehistoric people built a huge monument of stone pillars in England called Stonehenge. On the longest day of the year, the sun rises at the tip of a pillar called the Heel Stone. This day is called the summer solstice, the beginning of summer.

## Aris-who?

Aristarchus lived in Greece from 310 BC to 230 BC. People of his time believed the Earth was the center of the solar system. They also thought the sun was small. Today, we know it is 864,000 miles in diameter. But ancient people had only their eyes to judge the size of the sun. To most of them, the sun looked like a pretty small disk of brilliant light—exactly as it looks to you today.

*Don't be a fool. Follow this rule:*
*Never look directly at the sun!*

## Do our eyes deceive us?

Aristarchus knew that our eyes play tricks on us. Even huge objects, like the sun, look small if they are far away. You can experience the trick our eyes play any time. Just look at a tree or a building from far away. Frame it top to bottom between your hands. Now walk toward it while keeping it framed between your hands. You have to keep moving your hands farther and farther apart because it seems to grow! But of course, it's exactly the same size it always was.

# SUN FUN

## Shadow tricks

Aristarchus realized that the size of a shadow changes as an object gets closer or farther away from the light. Shadow tricks are easy. Put a lamp on a table near a bare wall. Take off the shade. Make shadows on the wall with your hand or other objects.

This will work best if the lamp is the only light in the room. Do the shadows of objects look like the real thing?

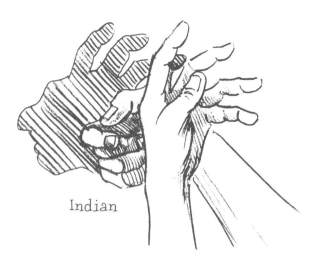

Indian

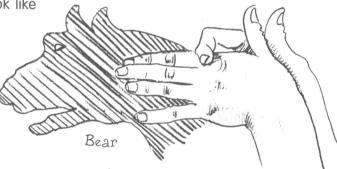

Bear

PIRATES

*Don't be a fool. Follow this rule:*
*Never watch a solar eclipse*
*without special equipment.*

## SUN FACT

In a *lunar* eclipse, the Earth gets
between the sun and the moon,
blocks the sun's light,
and casts a shadow on the moon.
It is safe to watch a lunar eclipse.
In a *solar* eclipse, the moon gets
between the Earth and the sun.
The moon is exactly the right size
and exactly the right distance
from the Earth to cover up
the surface of the sun.

## SUN FUN

### Like, a *total* eclipse, man!

By studying shadows, Aristarchus could tell you the size of a tree or building no matter where he stood. That's why he was able to figure out things about the sun when he saw the shadow of the Earth on the face of the moon during a lunar eclipse.

Can you make a lunar eclipse with your shadow lamp? Try using two different plates—a big one for the Earth and a small one for the moon. Ask a friend to help you line them up.

# SUN FUN

## Dial into the sun

The sun has been rising and setting for roughly five billion years. Some people say it's as regular as clockwork. Long before anyone built a mechanical clock with gears and springs and pendulums, people invented the sundial. This simple device let them tell the time of day just by the shadow of the sun.

## Materials

- ❑ a large or jumbo soda drink cup with its plastic cover and straw
- ❑ wristwatch or other portable clock
- ❑ black magic marker (permanent ink)
- ❑ pencil and tape

# Building it

Poke a hole in the side of the cup about two inches below the top. Use the pencil to make this hole. Put some stones in the bottom of the cup so it won't tip over. Put the plastic top on the cup. Push the straw through the hole in the top and the hole in the side. Have about a half-inch poking through the side. Tape this to the cup so it won't slip out. Maybe it's not gorgeous, but it's ready to use.

## SUN FACT

The straw is called a gnomon, from the Greek word *gnosis*, which means "one who knows." In this case, the gnomon knows the time of day.

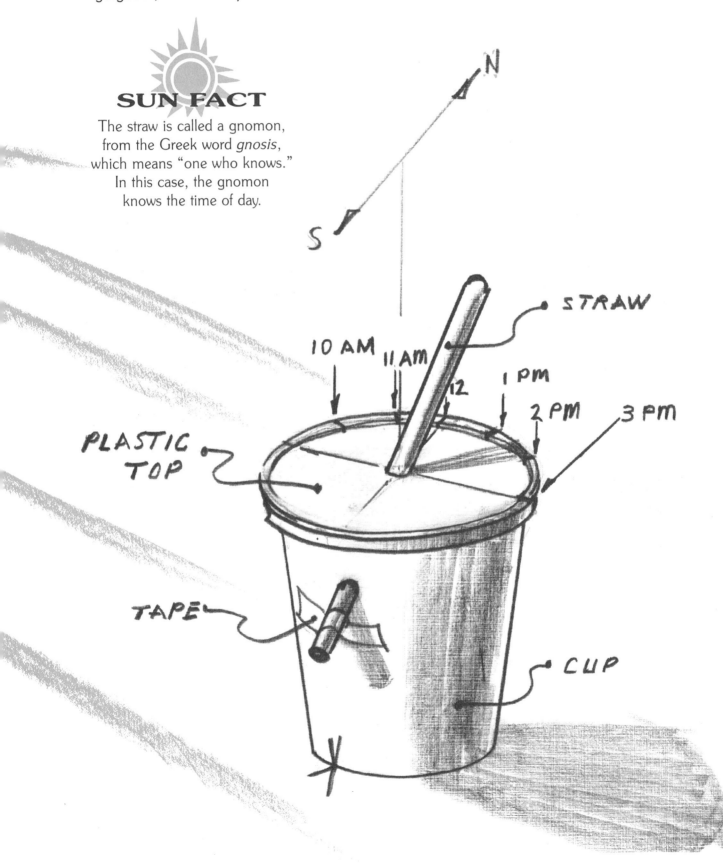

# Using it

Find a spot that's sunny from 10 AM until 3 PM. Put your sundial on the ground or a table. Be sure it is level. Find south. Now, turn your sundial cup until the straw points north. Once you have it set, be sure not to move it for the rest of the experiment. Make a mark on the side of the cup near the bottom and a mark on the ground or table. This will let you put the sundial back in the same place if it gets knocked over.

Beginning at 10 AM, use the magic marker to draw the shadow cast by the straw on the plastic top. Be neat and straight. Repeat this every hour until 3 PM. Leave your sundial out overnight. Next day, see if you can tell what time it is using your sundial instead of a clock.

# Understanding it

The shadow on your sundial moved from 10 AM to 3 PM in the same direction the hands of a clock move. So, the shadow moved clockwise. But if you did this experiment in the southern hemisphere, everything would change. The sun is in the northern sky. Shadows point south! Shadows move the opposite direction from the way they do in the northern hemisphere. That's why some people say, if clocks had been invented south of the border, they'd run backwards.

# The golden chariot travels two roads

In early Greek mythology, the sun was a god called Apollo who drove a fiery golden chariot along a heavenly road. Today, scientists know the sun isn't a fiery chariot. But the Greeks' chariot idea helped them learn important things about the sun. They observed that the golden chariot passed along a different road in the sky during different seasons of the year. In the winter, the sun travels a path low in the southern sky. But in the summer, the sun travels high overhead. With these basic facts, the Greeks invented solar architecture, which means designing buildings that use the sun for light and heat.

**SUN FACT**

Many different cultures believed the sun was a god.
The Egyptian name for the sun was Ra. The Inca called it Inti.
Mithra was the Persian god of the sun.
The Japanese thought the sun was a goddess called Amaterasu.
Why do you think so many people thought of the sun as a god?

27

## SUN FACT

It looks like the sun moves—but, in fact, it stays still.
It's the *Earth* that moves, spinning around its north-south axis.
One revolution takes 24 hours, causing day and night.
The Earth also moves around the sun in an orbit.
The trip around the sun takes one year.
During half of the Earth's orbit, the northern hemisphere
is tilted toward the sun, getting a lot of solar energy.
This causes summer. Gradually, the northern hemisphere
tilts away from the sun. Less solar energy reaches us,
the temperature drops, and it becomes winter.
Meanwhile, in the southern hemisphere,
summer has arrived.

## Solar or polar?

The Greeks built their houses of stone.
They didn't have glass for windows.
Imagine how cold your house would be
in winter with the windows open! Did the
early Greeks spend all winter shivering in
cold houses? No! At first, they burned wood.
Basically, they used the solar energy the trees
had saved up in their wood. But the Greeks
didn't take care of the forests by planting new
trees. When the supply of trees got low, there was an
energy crisis. Greek architects noticed that houses facing
south were more comfortable than houses facing any other direction.

That's because the winter sunshine filled the house and warmed
the air inside. It warmed the Earth floor and the thick walls,
keeping the people inside comfortable. So the Greeks realized
they could stay warm without burning up trees at all. They
just had to be sure that their houses faced south.

N.

EARTH'S SPIN

EARTH

- EQUATOR -

S.

# Keeping your cool

In Greece, winters are mild and summers are hot. When the Greeks solved the problem of keeping warm with the sun, they created a new problem in summer. With all that solar energy pouring in, the house got too hot! Something had to be done!

Solar architects knew they had to keep the hot sun out of the house. But how could they do that and still let the winter sun in? They thought about the two roads taken by the sun god, Apollo. They thought about shadows. They decided to build a *portico*, or covered porch, over the front of the house. During summer, the roof of the portico blocked the rays of the sun. The house stayed cool inside.

As fall approached, the days grew shorter and cooler. The sun travelled closer and closer to the horizon. More and more sunlight slipped under the portico, warming the inside. The careful design of the house worked automatically with the changing seasons.

## SUN FACT

Many other cultures invented solar architecture, including the ancient Chinese and the Pueblo Indians of the American Southwest. They built their cities up the sides of cliffs—the south sides! With one apartment stacked on top of another, everyone got equal amounts of sunshine. The Chinese used solar architecture in their temples. Windows were covered with rice paper, which glowed a beautiful golden color when the sun shone through it.

## SUN FUN

## Connect-the-dots portico

You can see how the portico worked if you connect the dots in this picture. Use a ruler. Connect all the matching numbers together. Pretend you are a sunbeam as you draw the lines. Color the sun and the lines in yellow. Color in the rest of the picture, too.

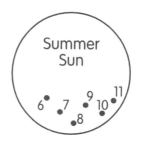

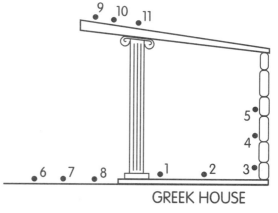

GREEK HOUSE

# SUN FUN

## A model project

What if you wanted to see how the portico works for real? First, you'd have to build a stone house. Then you'd have to watch it for a whole year. (That's how long the sun would take to change its path in the sky.) The sun simply won't speed things up just for scientists! This would be a very expensive experiment. And boring. (Of course, it also might be very exciting to build and then live in a stone house.)

So, scientists often make models of what they want to study. In this project, you will make a model Greek house. You'll pretend that a light bulb is the sun, so you'll be able to make the seasons change in an instant.

## Materials

❏ a box about 12" x 8" x 6"—A donut box works best (a shoebox will work well, too)

❏ plastic coffee creamers (empty and clean) or cardboard tubes from paper towel rolls

❏ table lamp (or even better, a spotlight)

❏ scissors, glue, and tape

❏ ruler

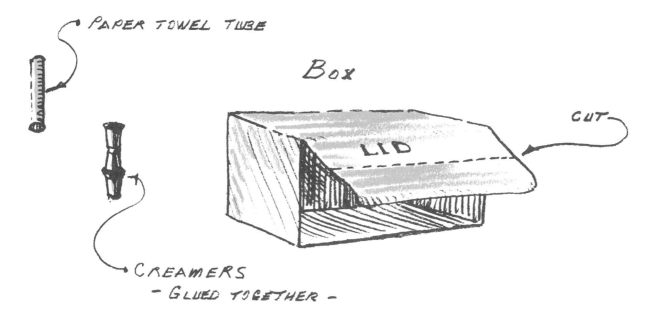

PAPER TOWEL TUBE

Box

LID

CUT

CREAMERS
- GLUED TOGETHER -

# Building it

Cut a slot in the backside of the box big enough for your hand to slip inside. Stand the box up on its front so the cover flap opens to make a portico. Trim any flaps off the sides of the cover. Fold the cover in half and cut along the crease. Now it is the right size for a portico.

You will need two pillars to hold the portico up. Measure how high the pillars have to be. Make them by gluing creamers together until they are the right height. (Or cut the paper towel tube to fit.) Attach the pillars with glue or tape. You might want to make a paper wall around your house to show the courtyard.

# Using it

Tape the model house to a table top. Have your helper hold the light about two feet in front of the house and one foot up in the air. Put your hand in the slot and turn on the light. Can you feel the warmth? Have your helper move the light three feet up. Now your hand is in shadow. Which position of the lamp is the summer sun?
Which one is winter?

# SUN FUN

## You can build a Greek Revival dog house

### Materials

- ❑ cardboard box
  (see instructions below)

- ❑ scissors or small saw
  (for big boxes)

- ❑ strong tape
  (like duct tape)

- ❑ ruler or yardstick

- ❑ waterproof paint

Cardboard boxes are sturdy, easy to work with, and fairly long-lasting. You will only need a small box for a mouse, hamster, or guinea pig. Cats and rabbits will want a bigger box— check at the grocery store. Dogs, unless they are very small, will need big boxes. Look for the kind televisions come in, or computers, or furniture. If you have a Saint Bernard, better keep an eye out for a refrigerator box! Whatever box you choose, it should be about the length of your pet on both sides. It should be about that tall, too.

Use a strong tape for construction. Scotch tape won't do. Duct tape is a good choice.

*WARNING!*
*Do not put your pets in the sun just so they can have a Greek Revival pet house. Make sure they have some other kind of shade to protect them from the sun.*

33

# Building it

**Step 1** Tape over where the flaps meet on the bottom.

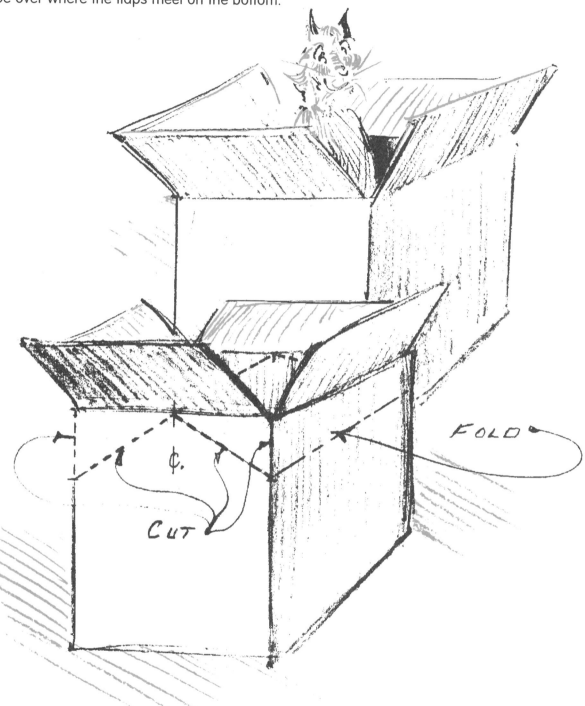

**Step 2** Make the roof peaks by marking the middle of the top front side. Measure from that mark to the edge. Divide this measurement in half, then make a mark that long down the front edge of the box. Draw a line between the two marks. Repeat on the opposite side. Cut the box down the edges to the marks, then cut away the triangles.

**Step 3** Fold the sides in at the edge marks to make a ceiling inside the house. Tape these together so they don't sag down on your pet. (If they won't stay up, just fold them all the way down inside. They will stiffen up the box.)

**Step 4** Make the door by drawing a line on the front between the two marks on the edges. Mark the middle of this line. Then on both sides of the mark, measure and mark halfway between the middle mark and the edges. Draw lines down to the bottom from these new marks. Cut out the door.

**Step 5** Make the roof and portico from another cardboard box. The roof will be as long as the box from peak to peak plus $\frac{3}{8}$ more again—that is the portico part. Measure from peak to peak, multiply this by three, then divide by eight. Add this number to the original measure to get the full length of the roof. Find out how wide the roof should be by measuring from the peak to the edge on the side. Multiply this by two. Use these measurements to mark out a piece of cardboard and cut it to size. Mark the middle of both ends to make the peak and fold along this line.

> NOTE: It is always easiest to fold cardboard if you place a ruler, yardstick, or board along the line you are folding.

**Step 6** Tape the roof securely to the other box.

**Step 7** Paint the house. Classic white? How about a stone pattern? Don't forget to paint your pet's name above the door. (A waterproof paint will make the cardboard last longer.) Pillars? Those are up to you. Use your ingenuity!

## Using it

When it is dry, find where you want to put it. Cats and hamsters and other small pets often stay in the house or a pen. Put their new house in their favorite sunny spot. For outside pets, be sure the house faces south. Set it up on some boards so the cardboard isn't touching the ground. A couple of rocks in the inside corners will keep it from blowing away. To make it last longer, cover the roof and sides with some heavy plastic from the hardware store.

Why not make a playhouse? You will definitely need big boxes. Maybe your friends will bring over their own Greek Revival playhouses. Then your backyard will look like a street in ancient Greece!

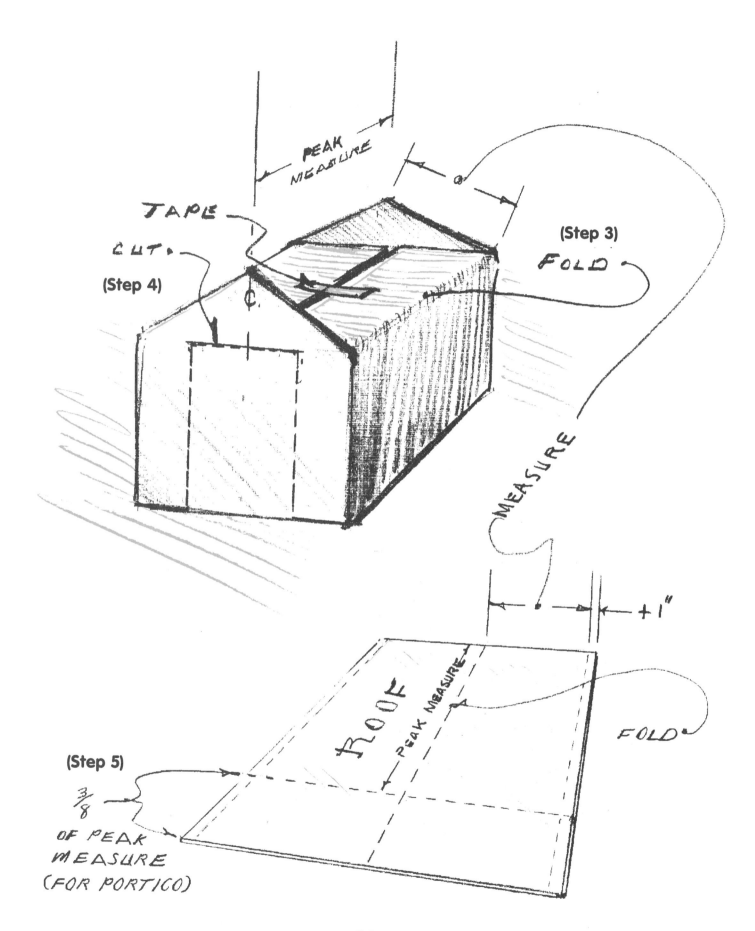

PEAK
MEASURE

TAPE

CUT.

(Step 4)

(Step 3)

FOLD

MEASURE

+1"

(Step 5)

$\frac{3}{8}$

OF PEAK
MEASURE
(FOR PORTICO)

ROOF

PEAK MEASURE

FOLD

# Luxury model

If you are handy with hammer, saws, nails, and wood, you might want to make your pet house out of plywood or boards. If you are not able to use these things yourself, ask an adult to help you. If you're lucky, you may find a wooden packing box! Whether you use cardboard or wood, the measurements are the same.

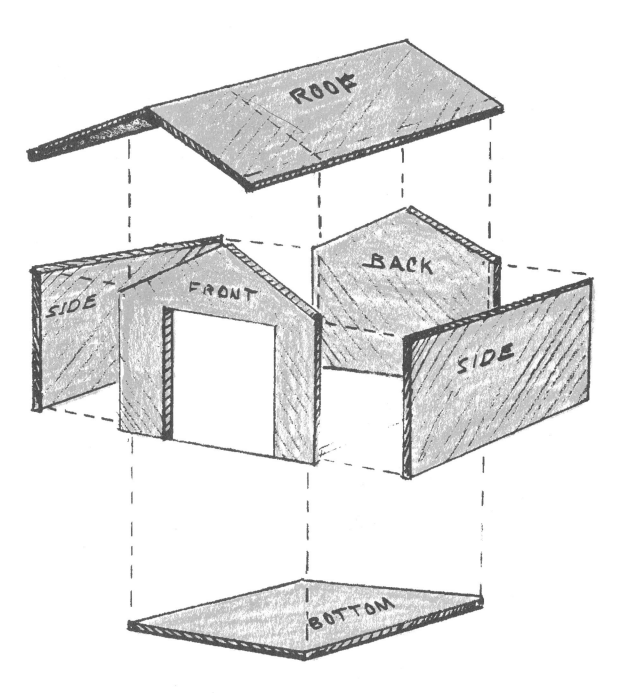

# 4
# A ROMAN ENERGY CRISIS

Do you like hot baths? Or those wonderful hot showers after playing hard at your favorite sport?

The Romans loved to go to the public baths. The public baths were like the health clubs of today, but without exercise machines. Roman citizens could soak in steaming pools. They played games, lifted weights, and wrestled in the huge, warm buildings. It took a lot of wood to keep enough fires going to heat the baths.

Soon, because the Romans did not replant the trees they cut down, the forests of Rome were gone. This led to an energy crisis. So the Romans studied what the Greeks had learned about keeping warm with solar energy. And they discovered something new—glass. Roman architects put big glass windows in the south walls of the bath houses. Because glass let the sunlight in without letting the heat out, the bath houses stayed much warmer. This saved a lot of wood!

# Greenhouses

The Romans put their new discovery to use in many ways. They built **greenhouses**. A greenhouse has a glass roof and glass walls. Solar energy warms the air inside, and the glass protects the interior from the cold. The Romans grew summer vegetables all winter long.

Pliny the Younger was a wealthy writer who lived in second-century Rome. He had a house in north central Italy, where winters are much colder than those in Greece. Because Pliny used glass in his windows, his home could be heated with solar energy. The glass trapped much more solar heat than stone walls alone. In fact, Pliny called his favorite room a *heliocaminus*—which means "solar furnace." Today, rooms like this are called "sun rooms."

**SUN FACT**

The Emperor Tiberius loved cucumbers. He ate one every day, even in winter. His gardeners grew them in miniature greenhouses called cold frames. The cold frames were on wheels so the gardeners could keep them in the sun all day long!

**SUN FACT**

The Romans were the first to pass laws to protect a citizen's right to sunshine, after some people built their heliocamini in front of their neighbors' glass-walled rooms.

# SUN FACT

The Earth's atmosphere acts like a big bubble of glass around our planet.
Sunlight comes through the atmosphere and warms up the Earth.
Just enough of this heat is trapped by the atmosphere so the
Earth stays comfortable. Scientists call this the "greenhouse effect."

## SUN FUN

## Test a deli-container greenhouse

Clear plastic works almost as well as glass at trapping solar heat. In this project, you will test how hot it can get inside a plastic deli-container. The deli-container will be a miniature greenhouse. There are many sizes and shapes of deli-containers— try a few different types to compare how well they work.

# Materials

❑ large square or rectangular plastic deli-container
(look for one with a clear top and black bottom—the kind that fast-food garden salads come in are often just right)

❑ black paint or black paper if your container is entirely clear

❑ thermometer

# Building it

If you have a clear container, paint the bottom black and let it dry. Or cut a piece of black paper to fit the bottom and tape it in place.

# Using it

Put your thermometer in the container and close it up. Be sure you can see the numbers. Record the temperature. Set the container in the sun. Noontime on a clear, still day will give you the best test results for this experiment. Let your greenhouse sit in the sun for a while, then check the temperature. Record this temperature, along with the outdoor temperature. Do this two more times, waiting about 10 minutes before you check again.

# Understanding it

Compare the temperatures you've written down. How hot can your greenhouse get? How long did it take to reach the hottest temperature? Which one worked the best?

NOTE: Save your biggest and best deli-container greenhouse. You will need it for another experiment at the end of this chapter.

# Old ideas in new houses

Today, we can use the ancient discoveries made by the Greeks and Romans to keep houses warm in winter and cool in summer. A modern house that uses these old ideas is called a "solar-tempered" home. This kind of house will face south. It has large windows on the wall facing the sun. The roof, like a portico, sticks out over the big windows. There may also be a greenhouse—or sun room—on the front of the house.

Even on the coldest winter day, the house will get all the heat it needs while the sun is shining. At night, or on cloudy days, the heat comes from a furnace. And on the hottest summer days, the house stays cool because the roof keeps sunshine out of the house.

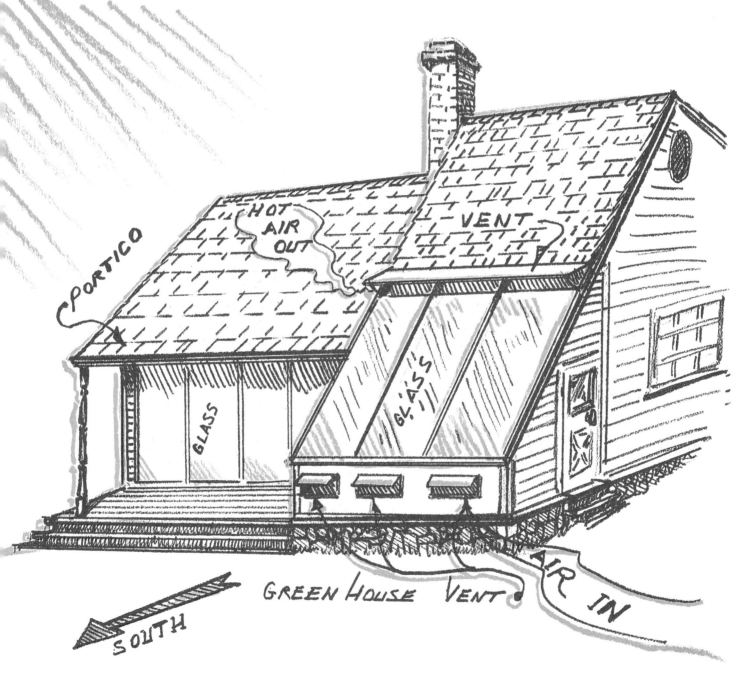

But the portico doesn't stop the sun from getting into the greenhouse. The sloped glass wall of the greenhouse sticks out into the sunshine because plants need light to grow, both in winter and summer. To make sure the greenhouse doesn't get too hot, it has special windows called vents. When the vents are open in summer, the solar energy escapes. In winter, the vents are closed, trapping the solar energy inside to keep the plants warm.

Solar-tempered homes use much less fuel in their furnaces and less electricity for air-conditioning. This means less pollution from power plants.

Solar houses have a long history in America. They were first built by the Pueblo Indians of the American Southwest and by the Anasazi Indians of New Mexico. The Anasazi built a city called Acoma, which means "sky city." It was much like the Greek city of Olynthia, with solar energy for every person who lived there. Today, there are more than 300,000 homes in the United States using solar energy for heat.

# SUN FUN

## Start your own seeds

At the spring equinox, it is often too cold to plant seeds outdoors. Most seeds like warm soil to start growing in, and tiny new plants need protection from the early spring chill.

In this project, you will find out if a greenhouse can help seeds and plants get a head start compared to seeds and plants that aren't grown in a greenhouse. You might want to grow your favorite vegetable, listed in "How Much Sunshine Can You Eat?" (See page 9.)

The test greenhouses you pick should have a tall top so you can leave plants in as long as possible once they start to grow.

To make a tall greenhouse, just stack the deli-containers on top of each other. Rectangular containers with flat tops and bottoms—like the ones McDonald's salads come in—work best for this. Simply cut out the flat part in the top of one and the bottom of another, then staple together. Be sure to leave some of the flat part for the staples. You can stack as many as you want this way.

44

## Materials

- ❏ your best deli-container greenhouse
- ❏ plant seeds—your favorites (how about some sunflowers and cucumbers?)
- ❏ several drink cups
- ❏ potting soil

## Building it

If the potting soil is dry, mix it in a bowl with water so it is damp, but not soggy.

Cut the drink cups all the way around, about two inches from the bottom.

Fill as many cups with soil as will fit in your greenhouse. Then plant your seeds in them. Plant them only as deep as the package says. Label each cup with the name of the plant you've put in it. Water your seeds lightly—don't make them soggy! Put the cups in your greenhouse and close it up.

Now make another set of seed cups with soil and seeds to match the ones in your greenhouse. You will use these to make comparisons. Put them in the bottom of a deli-container so they are easier to move around, but this time leave the top off.

## Using it

If you are doing this experiment when there is no danger of frost (late spring, summer, and early fall), then you can do it **outdoors**. Put your greenhouse in a spot that gets a lot of sun, but where it will not get knocked over by the wind. Put the other seed cups next to it.

If it is winter, or if frost is still likely, put your greenhouse **indoors** near a window that gets a lot of sun. Put the other seed cups near it, or in another window that gets just as much sun.

## SUN FACT

There are only two days in the year when daytime and nighttime both last 12 hours. The first occurs sometime near March 21 and is called the spring equinox. The other day is the autumnal equinox, which occurs around September 22.

Check your seed cups every day and record on the chart below what you observe. Be sure to water the seeds if they appear to dry out. (Which ones need more water—the ones in the greenhouse or outside it?) Once your seeds start growing, you will know whether or not the greenhouse gave them a head start.

Leave the plants in your greenhouse until they get too crowded—but be sure to put several holes in the container to let out the heat. If it is summer, you may have to open the top or your plants will cook!

You can end the experiment now. But if the season is right, why not grow some of your plants outdoors in the garden, or in some big flowerpots? Then you can find out exactly how many sun days your favorites take to grow from little seeds until they are ready to eat.

## Solar Graph for Mini-Greenhouse

| Date | Weather<br>Sun?<br>Clouds?<br>Wind?<br>Hot?<br>Cold? | Weather<br>Greenhouse | Outside | Observations<br>Seedlings appear?<br>How tall?<br>Greenhouse open or closed? | |
|------|------|------|------|------|------|
| | | | | Greenhouse | Outside |
| | | | | | |
| | | | | | |
| | | | | | |
| | | | | | |
| | | | | | |
| | | | | | |
| | | | | | |
| | | | | | |
| | | | | | |
| | | | | | |
| | | | | | |
| | | | | | |
| | | | | | |
| | | | | | |
| | | | | | |
| | | | | | |
| | | | | | |
| | | | | | |

# 5

# CATCHING SUNSHINE

When the summer sun is shining on a parking lot, would you walk on the blacktop with bare feet? No way, right? And you wouldn't touch a black car that's been parked in the sun, either. So you already understand a basic solar rule: Dark objects in sunshine **absorb** light and get very hot. The fact that light turns into heat when it is absorbed makes it possible for us to use sunshine as a fuel.

On the other hand, light is reflected off white and mirror-like surfaces. Objects like this absorb the least amount of solar energy. Because they **reflect** the light, these things stay cooler. That's why tennis players wear white clothes.

## SUN FACT

The temperature at the surface of the sun—called the photosphere—is about 10,000° Fahrenheit. A perfect reflector could recreate the temperature of the photosphere here on Earth.

47

## SUN FACT

If silver reflects and is supposed to stay cool, why does the metal slide at the playground get so hot? If you looked at the metal under a microscope, you would see pits and holes and dark spots. Some solar energy is absorbed by these flaws in the metal, and the slide warms up.

## SUN FUN

### Test the rule

Set a cast iron frying pan and a light-colored stone (about the size of a potato) in the sun on a window sill. Leave them there one hour. Now feel them. Which one is hotter? Does this prove the rule?

Now take the frying pan out of the sun. (Use pot holders—it might be too hot to hold!) Let it sit for one minute. Is it still warm?

The cast iron holds on to the solar energy it absorbed—just like the walls and floor of a Greek house. But eventually it gets cold. How long does that take?

Try this winter test on a not-too-cold, sunny day, around noontime. Put a thin black pan (a black pizza tray works well) and a white plate on the snow in the sun. What happens?

# Fire from the sun

Long ago, people learned that a curved piece of shiny metal aimed at the sun could light a fire. They called these things "burning mirrors." The ancient Chinese used them to light fires for religious purposes. They considered the light of the sun to be holy and pure, so fires made from sunlight had special meaning.

Early scientists dreamed of building solar weapons—like the laser beams and deathrays of science fiction—with burning mirrors. They thought they could sink ships and burn down castles with solar power. There is no real evidence, however, that anyone succeeded in using the sun for weapons.

## SUN FACT

The shape of reflector that works best is the curve called a parabola.
Big satellite dishes are parabolas, and the receiver is at the focus.
The reflector in a flashlight is also a parabola. The lens in a magnifying glass also works like a burning mirror, by focusing the sunlight to a point.

# A simple solar water heater

For most of human history, taking a bath was a complicated thing to do. People couldn't just turn on the faucet and have hot water come out. The water was mostly heated by wood fires. This meant you had to chop the wood, start the fire, then wait for the water to heat up before you could take a bath. Nobody just hopped in the shower.

About two hundred years ago, ordinary Americans discovered they could heat up bath water with sunshine. No fancy reflectors were needed. A metal tank and some black paint did the job just fine. In the morning, they filled the black tank with cold water. While the sun was shining, the tank absorbed solar energy and the water inside warmed up. By afternoon, the water was hot enough for a bath.

With this simple solar water heater, people could have hot water for a bath on any sunny day. Letting the sun heat the water was a lot easier than chopping wood!

## SUN FACT

Campers, hikers, and mountain climbers can have a hot shower anywhere in the world—they just have to take along a lightweight, black plastic bag with a shower head on it. They fill it up, hang it in the sun, and when the day is done, they can enjoy a nice hot shower. Not recommended for Polar Explorers!

## SUN FUN
## Solar squirt

A garden hose lying in the sun can make solar hot water. See for yourself. Turn the spray nozzle on the end of the hose off and the water faucet on. After the hose has been lying in the sun for a while, spray some water into a bucket. Check the temperature of the water in the bucket with a thermometer.

(Caution!! Never spray the water directly onto your hand—it's hot!)

 ## SUN FACT

Every year, the Olympic torch is lit by a burning mirror. This mirror is at the Temple of Hera in Olympia, Greece. After the torch is lit by the noonday sun in Olympia, it is carried by solar-powered athletes in a relay race. They run thousands of miles to wherever the Olympic Games are held.

 ## SUN FACT

In Golden, Colorado, there is a solar reflector that looks like a big saucer covered with 15 super-shiny mirrors. This "solar dish" powers a special hot-air engine that makes enough electricity from the solar heat to run 40 houses!

# SUN FUN

# Make your own mini solar water heater

Making a simple solar water heater is quick and easy. In the time it takes paint to dry, you'll be ready to try out this project.

## Materials

- ❏ empty soda can
- ❏ flat black paint
- ❏ wristwatch or other portable clock
- ❏ thermometer

## Building it

Paint the outside of an empty soda can black. Let it dry.

## Using it

Fill the soda can with cold water. Take the temperature of the water. Record this on the chart on page 54.

Set the can in the sun. Take the temperature every 15 minutes. Record the temperatures on the chart labeled "Mini Solar Heater." Don't forget to note the wind conditions, and whether the sun was shining or behind a cloud.

IMPORTANT: If it is a very windy or cold day, do this experiment indoors along a sunny window sill. Can you figure out why?

Feel the water. Make a note when it starts to feel warm, and then again when it feels warm enough to use for a bath.

NOTE: Remember to recycle! Airplanes are made out of aluminum because it is light and strong. Every three months, people in the United States throw away enough aluminum cans to rebuild all the commercial airliners currently in use.

# Understanding it

When the chart is full, you will have quite a bit of data about your mini-heater. Transfer this data to the grid below the chart. To do that, start with "time zero." Make a dot along the "time zero" line closest to the line for the temperature you measured. Do this with all the other time lines.

Connect all the dots with straight lines. Use a ruler so they will be neat. Now you have a picture of how your water heated up. Scientists call this picture a graph.

If you want to be really fancy, don't make dots, make circles. Use an open circle (○) if the day was sunny, a half-black circle (◑) if it was partly cloudy, and a black circle (●) if the sun was completely hidden by clouds. Now your graph tells you at a glance everything that's in your notes—except data about the wind. Can you think of a way to include the wind in the graph, too?

With this graph and your notes, you can answer questions like:

★ Did the temperature rise slowly and steadily?

☆ Did it rise quickly?

✳ Did it rise and fall?

☆ Did it reach a certain temperature, then stop?

✧ What is the hottest the water got?

Since all the heat is coming from the sun, see if the way the temperature acted matched what the sun was doing (shining or behind a cloud), and what difference a breeze made.

# Mini Solar Heater

## Simple Heater          Improved Heater

| Time | Weather Sun? Clouds? Wind? | Water Temp. | Outdoor Temp. | Weather Sun? Clouds? Wind? | Water Temp. | Outdoor Temp. |
|------|------|------|------|------|------|------|
| 0 | | | | | | |
| 15 | | | | | | |
| 30 | | | | | | |
| 45 | | | | | | |
| 1 Hr. | | | | | | |
| 15 | | | | | | |
| 30 | | | | | | |
| 45 | | | | | | |
| 2 Hr. | | | | | | |
| 15 | | | | | | |
| 30 | | | | | | |

# 6

# SOLAR ENERGY IN A PIZZA BOX

TAPE OR GLUE
SNACK BAGS (SHINY SIDE UP)
1" FROM
INSIDE EDGE

S'NACK-O'S

SNACK BAGS

PIZZA BOX

## HAVE YOU EVER . . .?

. . . thought of building a solar oven and baking S'mores with sunshine?

*Did you save a pizza carton in your solar junk box? If not, you should suggest pizza for supper tonight so you can start this project.*

Read the instructions carefully before you start. You've learned a lot about how to catch the sun to make heat. Try to imagine how the solar oven is supposed to work, even before you build one. And read the TIPS FOR SUCCESSFUL SOLAR COOKING at the end of this chapter. These helpful hints come from many young solar scientists who have already built and used a PIZZA BOX SOLAR OVEN.

## ☀ SUN FUN

### The pizza box solar oven

CUT THESE LINES

BOX HINGE

DO NOT CUT

$1\frac{1}{2}''$

$1\frac{1}{2}''$

— PIZZA BOX — SOLAR OVEN

## Materials

❑ one 14-inch (or medium-size) corrugated cardboard pizza box

❑ black construction paper

❑ extra-wide tinfoil or empty snack packages (potato chips, popcorn, etc.) with shiny foil on the inside. You need at least two large ones for the reflector flaps, and a bunch of small ones (or extra-wide tinfoil) to insulate the bottom.

❑ one sheet of clear plastic, a little bigger than the 14-inch pizza box (ask at the hardware store for crystal clear plastic window covering)

❑ glue, tape, ruler (a yardstick is best), magic marker, scissors or an X-acto knife (if an adult is helping you)

❑ a dark metal tray (if you have one in the kitchen) that fits inside the pizza box (or try the black plastic bottom from a deli-container)

# Building it

**Step 1** Cut the sealed ends off the snack bags, then cut them open along the seam. Wipe off the oil and crumbs on the shiny side with a paper towel. Work carefully—don't tear the bags.

**Step 2** Open the 14-inch box. Clean out any crumbs or dried bits of cheese. Cover the bottom with snack bags, shiny side up. Leave a one-inch space between the bags and the sides of the box. Glue or tape them in place.

**Step 3** Cover the snack bags with the black construction paper. Glue or tape the paper into place. Do not go up the sides of the box with the paper.

**Step 4** Close the box. On the top of the box, measure 1½ inches in from the edge and make a mark. Do this in several places all around the top. Now draw a line along these marks to make the outline of the flap. Note where the hinge of the box is. Write "DO NOT CUT" along the line near the hinge.

**Step 5** Cut along the front and two side lines to make the flap. Work carefully. If you are using scissors, you can get started by poking a hole with a pencil in the corner where two lines meet. Be sure to turn the corners when you're cutting . . . you'll ruin your box if you cut to the edges! And remember not to cut along the line that will be the hinge of the flap.

**Step 6** (It helps to have a partner for this part.) Place your ruler along the uncut line that marks the hinge of the flap. Gently pry open the flap. Make the fold on the hinge crisp and neat.

**Step 7** Cut one of the big snack bags to the size of the flap. Spread glue on the side of the flap that faces into the box. (Don't use big globs of glue—it will squish out and make a mess. Thin, squiggly lines of glue work best.) Glue the bag to the flap with the shiny side up. Flatten out all the wrinkles. Wipe up any glue smears with a damp paper towel before they dry.

SNACK BAG

FLAP

FLAP-HINGE UP

57

**Step 8** Close the box. Put it on the sheet of plastic. Draw the outline of the box on the plastic with the magic marker. Remove the box.

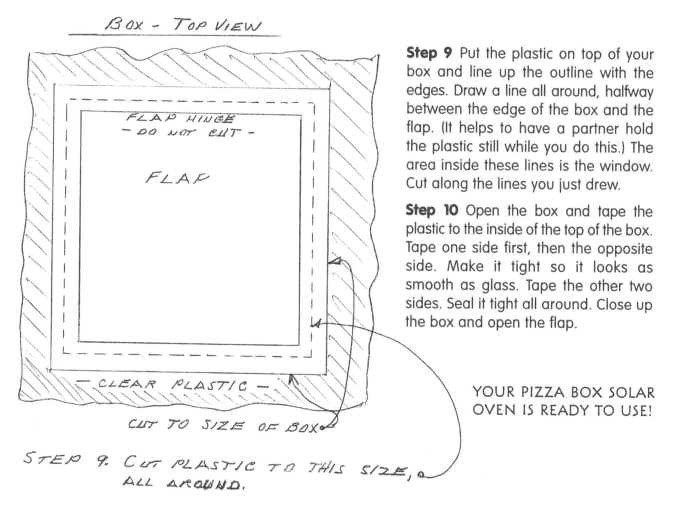

BOX - TOP VIEW

FLAP HINGE
— DO NOT CUT —

FLAP

— CLEAR PLASTIC —

CUT TO SIZE OF BOX

STEP 9. CUT PLASTIC TO THIS SIZE, ALL AROUND.

**Step 9** Put the plastic on top of your box and line up the outline with the edges. Draw a line all around, halfway between the edge of the box and the flap. (It helps to have a partner hold the plastic still while you do this.) The area inside these lines is the window. Cut along the lines you just drew.

**Step 10** Open the box and tape the plastic to the inside of the top of the box. Tape one side first, then the opposite side. Make it tight so it looks as smooth as glass. Tape the other two sides. Seal it tight all around. Close up the box and open the flap.

YOUR PIZZA BOX SOLAR OVEN IS READY TO USE!

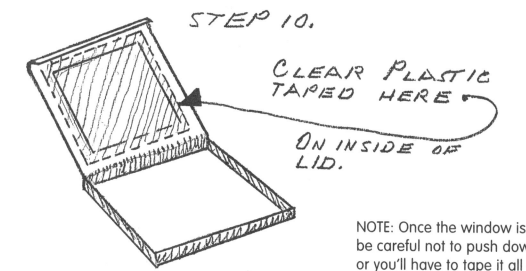

STEP 10.

CLEAR PLASTIC TAPED HERE

ON INSIDE OF LID.

NOTE: Once the window is in place, be careful not to push down on the flap or you'll have to tape it all over again!

# Using it

# How to make solar S'mores

**Ingredients:**

❑ graham crackers

❑ marshmallow fluff

❑ Hershey's® milk chocolate bar

**To make:** Break graham crackers in half. Put a blob of fluff in the center. Place two squares of the chocolate bar on top. The solar S'more is ready to cook. (Note: Do not put another graham cracker on top as you would for regular S'mores. Can you guess why?)

# Baking with the sun

Pick a day with bright sun, few clouds, and not too much wind. Make up some solar S'mores. Put your Pizza Box Solar Oven in the sun. Put the S'mores on the dark tray, if you have one, or set them on the black paper. (To keep the paper clean, first put a piece of clear food wrap under the S'mores.) Then put your thermometer in.

**REMEMBER: NEVER LOOK DIRECTLY AT THE SUN!!**

*GOT YOUR SUNGLASSES?*

Aim the oven at the sun and adjust the flap to reflect the most sunlight in on your S'mores. You can tell the aim is just right when the shadow of the flap lines up with marks you drew on the top of the box. You can tell the flap is adjusted correctly by looking for the sun's reflection inside the oven. Most flaps make a bright band of sunlight. This will be the hottest spot. You can find it by moving your hand around over the window. Try to make this hot reflection shine on your S'mores. Hold the flap at the best angle. (Don't want to hold the flap? Can you hold it in place with a string? How about a stick, or a straw?)

Wait a few minutes. Is the chocolate getting shiny? What does that mean? Make a note of the temperature, then open the box and test if the S'more is done. If the chocolate is all gooey when you touch it, it's time to eat and maybe cook s'more!

*BE CAREFUL IF YOU ARE USING THE DARK TRAY. IT'S HOT! USE A POT HOLDER TO TAKE IT OUT.*

# SUN FUN

## Don't snooze while the S'mores are cooking

While the S'mores are cooking, check out this list of solar energy principles. If you can't remember what each word means, look back in the previous chapters. Circle the solar energy principles used by your solar oven.

- ★ **renewable**
- ☆ **solstice**
- ✴ **greenhouse**
- ☆ **solar-tempered**
- ✪ **absorb**
- ☆ **portico**
- ★ **equinox**
- ✭ **reflect**

# Tips for using the pizza box solar oven

The use of a dark metal pizza tray is highly recommended for best results. The metal heats up hotter than the black paper alone—it **absorbs** solar energy better!

If you can help it, do not use the thin, grayboard type of pizza box. These rip easily, and because they do not have trapped air like corrugated cardboard, they don't hold in the heat very well. If you do have to use this kind, be very careful as you cut things out, and be especially careful as you fold the flap.

For neatness and ease of assembly, be sure the snack bag you use for the flap is big enough to cover it in one continuous piece.

Sometimes, white glue will not hold the snack bag material to the cardboard very well. If the foil on the flap starts to peel off, tape around the edges to hold it in place. If this doesn't work, try a stronger glue. Snack bags not working out? Try tinfoil. Be sure to use the shiny side!

Set up the oven on blacktop, brick, or cement, close to the south side of a building. Shelter the oven from any winds.

Try to tilt the oven up a little on the north side, but not so much that the food slides off the tray. This helps get rid of the shadows cast by the edges of the box.

# 7
# SOLAR HOT WATER DAY & NIGHT

### HAVE YOU EVER . . .?

. . . blown on a cup of hot chocolate to cool it down? What happens?

The wind is like the breath of the sun. When it blows over a simple solar water heater, the water in the tank just can't get hot enough for a bath.

In 1891, an American inventor named Clarence M. Kemp solved that problem so people could count on having solar hot water more often. Mr. Kemp knew what the Romans had discovered about glass, so he put the tank inside a miniature greenhouse. The water in his improved solar heater warmed up faster, got hotter, and stayed warm even after the sun went down.

# SUN FUN

## Improve your mini solar water heater

In this project, you will do the same kind of test that Mr. Kemp did over one hundred years ago. Will your results be the same?

## Materials

- ❑ your mini solar water heater
- ❑ a deli-container greenhouse big enough to hold the soda can (Look for one that holds a whole roasted chicken or a clear, quart-size salad container, or a shoebox with a plastic window in the cover—or use the method described in "Start Your Own Seeds" on page 44.)
- ❑ wristwatch or other portable clock
- ❑ thermometer

## Using It

Fill the soda can with cold water. Take the temperature. Record this on the chart labeled "Mini Solar Heater" (on page 54, under "Improved Heater").

Put the full can in the deli-container. Make a hole through the plastic for your thermometer. This way, you can take the temperature in the can without opening the greenhouse. Put the experiment in the sun. Be sure the clear side is facing the sun.

NOTE: You could do this experiment outside on a windy day. The greenhouse protects your simple water heater from the wind and cold, just as the cold frame protected the Emperor's cucumbers.

### DON'T LOOK AT THE SUN.
*You can tell the container is aimed just right when its shadow falls directly behind it.*

Measure and record the temperature every 15 minutes just as you did before (review instructions on page 52). Once you have all the data, transfer it to the same graph you used to test your simple solar water heater. Use a different colored pen or pencil to make the marks, and draw the connecting line in this same color.

Did your improved solar water heater get hotter, faster, just like Mr. Kemp's? You can tell at a glance. Look at the graph and ask yourself: Which color line is above the other one? If that color belongs to the improved heater, then that one worked the best.

Review the questions we asked earlier about the simple solar heater. Are the answers different for the improved version?

## Something really impressive

Can you think of a way to add insulation to your improved water heater? If you can, maybe you should run another test to see if it works even better. Use a third color to record the results on your graph. Now you have a graph that tells quite a story. It would impress solar scientists everywhere!

It would also make a great display for a science fair. Be sure to include each version of your mini-solar heater and make signs that explain things to people who stop by.

# Hot water around the clock

Even Mr. Kemp's improved solar water heater cooled off overnight. There were no early-morning solar showers until the invention of the **flat plate collector**. This device was the key to solar-heated water around the clock. A flat plate collector is a large, shallow metal box. The inside is painted black. The collector has a glass cover. The sides and bottom are surrounded with insulation. Black pipes snake over the bottom.

The flat plate collector sits on a roof that faces south. A pipe for cold water connects to the bottom. Another pipe connects to the top. Both of these pipes go into the house and connect to a tank full of water. This tank is covered, top to bottom and all around, with a thick blanket of insulation.

The pipes are not very large, so when the sun shines on them, they heat up quickly. The cold water comes into the pipes at the bottom of the flat plate collector. Since there is only a tiny amount in each pipe, the water heats up quickly, too. By the time it goes out the top pipe, it is hot enough to scald you.

**SUN FACT**

William J. Bailey designed the first flat plate collector in 1909. His solar water heater was called the "Day & Night."

66

From the collector, the hot water goes into the big tank. There, it mixes with the cold water. This makes the whole batch of water a little warmer, but not quite warm enough. So back it goes into the bottom of the collector. Each time the water goes through the collector, the whole tankful gets warmer and warmer—as long as the sun is shining.

Eventually, the tank of water is just the right temperature for baths. It can take as little as three hours of sunshine to heat up the tankful of water. The insulation keeps the water hot around the clock—24 hours a day.

## SUN FACT

Solar hot water is not just for homes. A hotel in Eilat, Israel, uses flat plate collectors to heat water for the guests. A swimming complex near Tokyo, Japan, heats the pool water with solar energy. An apartment building in Burlington, Vermont, has collectors on the roof to help heat the water used by the residents.

## SUN FUN

## Water magic

Most things shrink when they freeze, but not $H_2O$. If you haven't noticed how water expands when it freezes, try this: Fill an ice tray to the brim. Set it in the freezer overnight. Check in the morning. Are the ice cubes higher than the rim of the tray?

# A little design change for winter

In 1913, a freak cold spell hit California. The temperature dropped to a record low of 20°F. The pipes in the Day & Night solar water heaters popped like popcorn. Water leaked into people's houses. The disaster nearly put Mr. Bailey out of business.

To save his business, Mr. Bailey changed the design so that the pipes from the collector went into a coil of pipe inside the water tank. This closed loop was filled with an alcohol/water anti-freeze mixture. So even on freezing nights, the pipes in the collector were safe. By inventing the closed loop, Mr. Bailey gave the world solar hot water around the clock all year long!

## SUN FACT

Ninety percent of the homes on Cyprus have solar water heaters. Sixty-five percent of homes in Israel do. Thirty percent in Australia. But only 1.5 percent of the homes in the United States have solar water heaters. Americans in 98.5 million homes still pollute the air to get themselves clean!

## SUN FUN

### Put solar on your house

An architect designs houses. A **solar architect** designs houses that use solar energy, like the one on page 42. You can be a solar architect, too.

Draw a diagram of your house. Show all the rooms. Now draw a flat plate collector on the roof. Draw pipes to all the places you use hot water in your house. Don't forget the washing machine!

Color the pipes red. Then it will be easy to see where all that solar hot water is going. Is there a place to put a greenhouse? Draw one.

# 8

# HEATING HOUSES WITH THE SUN

### HAVE YOU EVER . . .?

... been in a room that gets roasting hot when the sun shines—even in winter?

You probably had to open the windows to stay comfortable. What a waste to let all that clean solar heat go out the window! A solar architect would find a way to save it up for nighttime.

Just think of what the winter weather is like in places where houses need the most heat—stormy, cloudy, snowy, windy, and cold cold cold.

The ancient Greeks were able to heat their houses fairly well by facing them into the sun and adding porticos. But during a winter in Greece, the temperature rarely fell below freezing. This is not the case in New England, Montana, Oregon, or the mountains of Colorado. And that's where solar architects wanted to build solar houses.

Thanks to the Romans, the use of glass to trap solar energy helped architects get closer to designing a completely solar-heated house. But even with big front windows and greenhouses, the modern solar-tempered house still cooled down at night.

Solar architects had the same kind of problem that people have had at harvest times throughout the centuries. All at once, the tomatoes are ready, the wheat is ready, the melons and squash and potatoes—everything is ready to pick at once. But no one can eat it all! In a solar house, a sunny day is like harvest time.

To save the heat from a sunny day, solar architects learned to build a **solar heating system**. A solar heating system does three things:

1. Collects solar energy while the sun shines.

2. Stores solar energy as heat.

3. Moves the heat from storage into the house to keep the rooms warm day or night.

## SUN FACT

The Massachusetts Institute of Technology was a leader in solar house heating research. Scientists worked there from 1938 until 1962 testing solar houses. They built four houses and proved that the sun could supply half the heat needed by a house in the cold climate of Massachusetts.

Alaska

## A solar map

Color in this map of the United States. Use red, pink, orange, and yellow crayons. Now you have a picture of where the sun shines hottest and longest—all the red and pink places! The next best places for solar energy are orange. If you live in the U.S., what color do you live in?

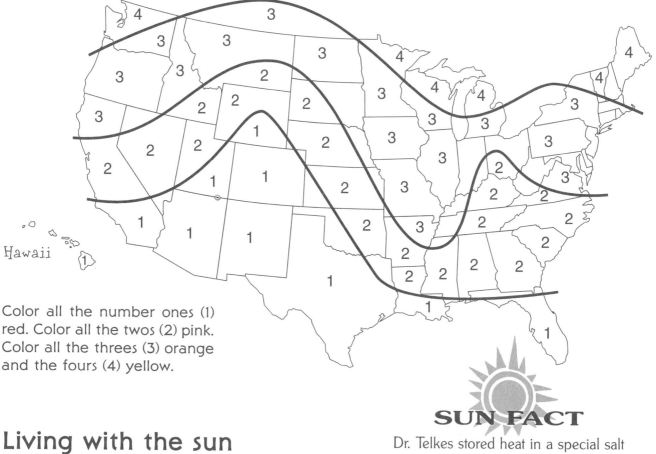

Hawaii

Color all the number ones (1) red. Color all the twos (2) pink. Color all the threes (3) orange and the fours (4) yellow.

# Living with the sun

## Dr. Maria Telkes

Dr. Maria Telkes was one of the scientists who worked at the Massachusetts Institute of Technology. Her colleagues were trying to store solar heat in huge water tanks, but she had her own ideas about a better way to store heat.

**SUN FACT**

Dr. Telkes stored heat in a special salt solution called Glauber's salts, which absorbed enormous amounts of heat. While other scientists needed 17,000 gallons of water to store enough heat to keep their solar houses warm, Dr. Telkes only needed 1,000 gallons of Glauber's salts.

In 1948, Dr. Telkes convinced a wealthy Boston lady, Amelia Peabody, to build a solar house in Dover, Massachusetts. It would be the first one entirely heated by the sun. Amelia Peabody's architect, Eleanor Raymond, designed the house and Dr. Telkes designed the solar heating system.

Today we wouldn't find it strange that a woman architect, a woman scientist, and a woman financier worked together on such an exciting project. But in their day, all these women were aiming toward new horizons when most people thought the only place for women was in the home.

Dr. Telkes' solar house worked well for three years, but then the salts failed. Amelia Peabody had to put in a regular furnace. Even so, Telkes' ideas were the most advanced of her time.

## SUN FACT

Dr. Telkes was a tireless solar pioneer. She was also a great cook. One November day in New York City, she served several guests a solar lunch entirely cooked in a box oven she designed. In less than thirty minutes, out came a cast iron pan with nine sizzling hamburgers and onions, a pot of potatoes, and a pot of vegetables.

# A very big water heater

One type of solar heating system is like a giant solar hot water heater. Several flat plate collectors are put on the roof of a house. The roof has to face south.

The water that flows through the collectors comes from a huge tank in the basement of the house. While the sun shines, pumps push the water through the pipes of the collectors. All day long, the water gets hotter and hotter. The tank is so well insulated that it can stay warm for many days—even if the sun doesn't shine. At night, no water flows into the collectors. Instead, the hot water in the tank is pumped to radiators in the house. The radiators release the stored solar heat into the air, and the house warms up. There is so much hot water in the tank that it only cools down slightly during the night.

FLAT PLATE COLLECTOR

PUMP

HOT-WATER TANK

# Stormy days

The water stored in the tank is very hot. It will be able to heat the house for many days, rain or shine.

But what if clouds hang around for a week, and the water gets cold? Another source of heat, called **back-up heat**, must be used until the sun shines again. The back-up heat can come from an oil or propane or wood furnace.

# Living with the sun

## A solar school

The first solar-heated public building was the Rose Elementary School in Tucson, Arizona, built in 1948.

The school's solar collector not only caught sunshine—it also kept the rain out of the school. The collector was the roof of the school, made of aluminum troughs laid side by side. The top was painted black. Air from the rooms was blown through the troughs by fans. When the sun was shining, the air heated up, then went back into the rooms. Everyone inside stayed cozy.

Winter temperatures in Tucson rarely go below 50°F, so it didn't take much solar energy to keep the rooms comfortable. This simple solar heating system supplied nearly all the heat needed by the school.

## SUN FACT

High school students in Oxford, Massachusetts, designed and built a greenhouse at their school. Inside the greenhouse were 2,000 gallons of water for storing solar heat. The computer class designed automatic computer controls and monitoring devices for the greenhouse's solar system.

# America's first solar village

Wisconsin is far north, has bad winters, and the weather is often cloudy. It's the kind of state where many people think solar energy won't work. But the citizens of Soldier's Grove, Wisconsin, didn't believe that. In 1978, they made a law that new buildings had to get half their heat from solar energy. Since that year, over twenty businesses, the Community Library, the Post Office, an elderly housing complex, and several homes have been built in town. All of them get at least half their heat from the sun.

Another place with very cold winters is Snowmass, Colorado. Amory Lovins lives there in the Rocky Mountain Institute, which is both his house and an energy laboratory. He believes we can run the entire world on clean, renewable energy. To demonstrate this, the Institute gets all its heat, hot water, and electricity from the sun. Amory Lovins grows bananas in his greenhouse. He picks ripe ones in the middle of the winter!

**SUN FACT**

Just as the Romans did so long ago, the citizens of Soldier's Grove passed sun laws. These laws make sure that one person can't take away another person's sunshine by building too high, or by planting trees that would shade someone else's solar heating system.

# INSULATION

## SUN FUN

### Find the best insulation

Solar-heated houses in places like Wisconsin would not be possible without insulation. Solar-heated water could not stay warm overnight if the tank were not insulated. Insulation is almost as important for solar heat as the sun is!

Fiberglass insulation comes in big pink rolls, like thick blankets, and is used in the walls of houses. Inside the walls or roofs of houses (or wrapped around the hot water tank), these blankets trap the heat that is trying to escape to the outdoors. If you squashed the blanket flat, however, it wouldn't work. It's not the fiberglass that stops the escape of heat; it's all the little pockets of air trapped in the blanket. Heat does not move very easily through tiny air spaces.

Many different things make good insulation. In this project you will build an insulation test chamber. With it, you'll be able to test different things and see how well they keep the heat in a cup of hot water.

Check in your solar junk box for things like packing peanuts, take-out bags (tear them up and make tiny crumpled paper balls), bubble pack, and cotton balls saved from vitamin and medicine bottles. Got any milkweed fluff? Test as many things as you like. In fact, you might want to build more than one test chamber, or invite a friend to bring one over.

## Materials

- ❏ 2 small paper hot drink cups with one plastic top (Paper coffee cups work best. Avoid styrofoam: the chemicals used to make it destroy the ozone layer.)

- ❏ 1 quart-size yogurt, cottage cheese, or similar deli-container with top

- ❏ white rice, Rice Krispies, and various other things to test as insulation

- ❏ thermometer

- ❏ timer or clock

## Building it

Center the top of one of the small hot drink cups on the plastic lid of the yogurt container. Draw the outline. Cut out the circle slightly inside the line. Your insulation test chamber is set to go.

QUART SIZE CONTAINER WITH LID.

PLASTIC LID

YOGURT

PLASTIC LID

# Using it

First, get the control case. ("Control" is a word scientists use. It means the part of an experiment where the scientist sees what would happen if he or she hadn't fooled around with things in the first place. For this project, that means finding out how fast the water cools down in a plain cup without insulation.)

Fill a small cup with hot water from the tap. Put the cover on. Slip the thermometer in. Write down the temperature on the chart in the "time zero" box under "Control." Check the temperature every five minutes and write down the number in the correct box. Be sure to wiggle the thermometer to stir up the water before you read off the temperature.

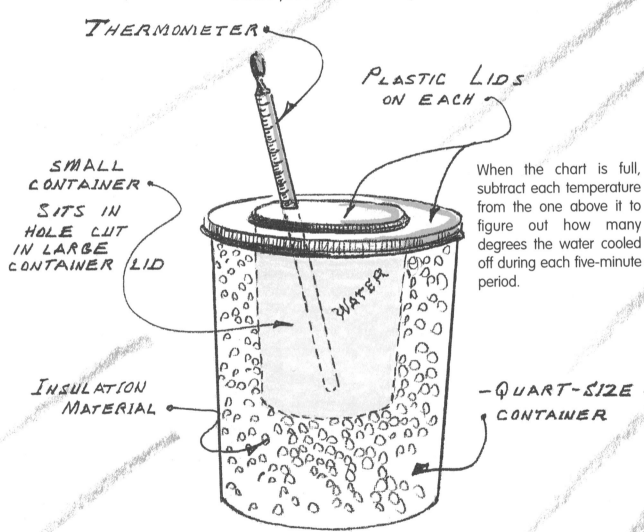

THERMOMETER

PLASTIC LIDS ON EACH

SMALL CONTAINER SITS IN HOLE CUT IN LARGE CONTAINER LID

WATER

When the chart is full, subtract each temperature from the one above it to figure out how many degrees the water cooled off during each five-minute period.

INSULATION MATERIAL

QUART-SIZE CONTAINER

Next, try the rice. Pour some into the test chamber. Set the small cup in. If the small cup isn't even with the rim of the container, pour some more rice in the bottom. When you get the cup even with the rim, fill in around the sides. Use the cover to keep the rice from dropping into the cup.

Put on the big top. Fill the other small cup with hot tap water, put on the top, and slide it into the test chamber. Slip the thermometer in. Write down the temperature at "time zero" under "Rice" on the chart. Check the temperature every five minutes and write down that number in the correct box.

Repeat the above with Rice Krispies, and then with different things you choose.
Test as many as you like. Compare your charts and think about these questions:

☆ Which materials worked the best?

★ Is there anything the best ones share in common?
Are they light, heavy, in strands, in chunks, fluffy, or dense?

☆ Did any of the test materials let the water get colder than the control?
Better think of a different name for that stuff than insulation!

NOTE: What's most important in this experiment is how many degrees the water cools down every five minutes. That information tells us how well the material works as insulation. The better the insulation, the fewer degrees the water cools down each time.

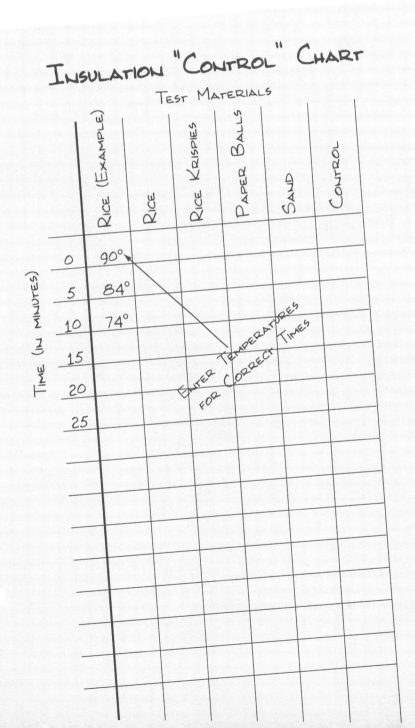

INSULATION "CONTROL" CHART

TEST MATERIALS

TIME (IN MINUTES)

| | RICE (EXAMPLE) | RICE | RICE KRISPIES | PAPER BALLS | SAND | CONTROL |
|---|---|---|---|---|---|---|
| 0 | 90° | | | | | |
| 5 | 84° | | | | | |
| 10 | 74° | | | | | |
| 15 | | | | | | |
| 20 | | | | | | |
| 25 | | | | | | |

ENTER TEMPERATURES FOR CORRECT TIMES

# Here's a challenging design problem

Heat rises. But the top of our test chamber, where most of the heat will escape, is not insulated at all. Can you design a test chamber that lets you put the insulation over the top, as well as the bottom and sides? Remember, you will need some way to check the temperature every five minutes without uncovering the cup.

**SUN FACT**

Do you ever read a newspaper twice? It takes trees 20 years to grow, but we toss out the newspapers made from them after just a few minutes of reading. Over 500,000 trees are used in every Sunday edition—an entire forest! One way to give old newspapers new life is to use them for insulation. If the paper is ground up, then blown between the walls in houses, it will save energy for decades!

# Solar energy in the city

The Greeks could heat a city with solar energy 2,000 years ago—can we do it today? A project on Thompson Street in North Philadelphia gives us a glimpse of what the solar city of the future might look like.

The north side of a row of 23 attached houses faces the street. They look just like ordinary city houses. But on the south side, every room has windows that let in light and solar heat. One part of the south wall is a huge flat plate solar collector, which makes hot air from sunshine. The solar rowhouses use 63 percent less heat from a furnace than the regular rowhouses just across the street, and the fuel bills of the people in the solar houses are half as much. Better yet, they're causing only half as much pollution!

## SUN FACT

Solar heat collectors built into the wall of a house are called "trombe walls." The Philadelphia rowhouses have concrete behind the glass to absorb the sun. Other trombe wall designs use tubes or barrels of water.

## SUN FACT

Skyscrapers cast huge shadows on the buildings way down below them. If only someone had thought to make Sun Laws when American cities were growing!

# 9
# TIME TO TURN UP THE HEAT

What do you do when you want something to cook faster on a regular kitchen stove? You turn up the heat with a twirl of the dial. But we can't turn up the sun!

The PIZZA BOX SOLAR OVEN you built earlier probably reached a temperature of about 150°F. That was good enough to cook solar S'mores, but not much else. Pizza, for instance, is often cooked at 400°F! So if we want to cook other fast foods like pizza, nachos, or tacos, we've got to find a way to turn up the heat.

The temperature a solar oven reaches depends on how much sunshine goes into it and how well the heat stays in there (and, of course, how well-made the oven is). The window lets in a certain amount of sunshine. The flap is the same size as the window, and reflects most of the sun aimed at it into the box. That's like having two windows of sun in one place. Twice as much solar energy means twice as much heat.

Overlapping sunshine like this is the only way to increase the solar heat available in a fixed area like the oven.

## SUN FACT

On average, about 1,000 watts of solar energy fall on a 3' × 3' patch of ground—about the size of a sidewalk square. That's enough power to light ten 100-watt light bulbs!

## SUN FUN

# Let's make a *two-flapper* solar oven

In this project, you will nest the Pizza Box Solar Oven inside another pizza box. This will make another reflector flap. It will also give us space to put some insulation around the sides of the oven. With much more sun pouring in, and insulation helping to hold in the heat, the temperatures ought to be impressive.

In fact, the temperature will be high enough to cook mini-pizzas, nachos, or tacos!

## Materials

❑ Pizza Box Solar Oven from chapter 6

❑ 16"-18" pizza box

❑ the same materials you used in chapter 6, except for the clear plastic (page 56)

## SUN FACT

Scientists say the amount of sun falling on a given spot is equal to One Sun. If we have a reflector or magnifying glass that doubles the sunshine on that spot, scientists say the spot is now getting the energy of Two Suns. So the two-flapper is a Three-Sun oven!

## Building it

**Step 1** Center the oven on top of the bigger pizza box. Draw its outline. Set the oven aside. Note where the hinge of the big box is. Write "DO NOT CUT" along the line near the hinge.

**Step 2** Follow the instructions for Steps 1, 2, 5, 6, and 7 in chapter 6 (page 55).

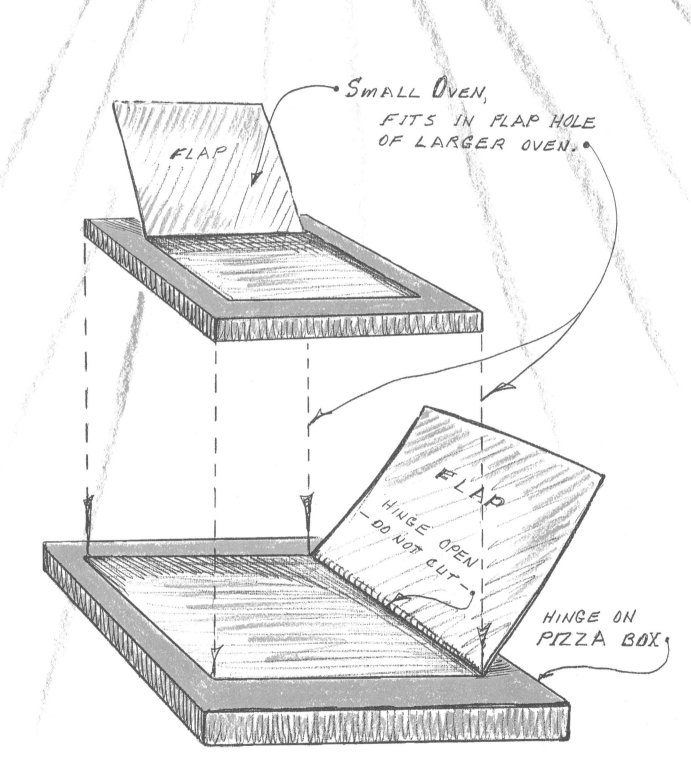

SMALL OVEN, FITS IN FLAP HOLE OF LARGER OVEN.

FLAP

FLAP

HINGE OPEN — DO NOT CUT

HINGE ON PIZZA BOX

**Step 3** Open the big flap. Set the oven over the hole so that when both flaps are open, they are side by side. Press the oven into the hole. It should be a snug fit.

**Step 4** Fold both flaps all the way open. Set the whole assembly upside down on a table. Open the big box bottom. Tape the corners of the little flaps on the big box top.

**Step 5** Fill in the spaces with insulation. (Pick one that worked best from your insulation test chamber experiments—one that will be easy to stuff in the spaces.)

## DID YOU NOTICE?

Corrugated cardboard is insulation. Look at the edge. See the wavy line of paper between the other two layers? Air is trapped in the spaces. Trapped air is good insulation. Why did we put foil **under** the black paper? What could it be reflecting there?

**Step 6** Close the bottom. Turn right side up. Tape the big box shut. (If your oven is loose, tape it to the big box, too.)

**Step 7** Set the two flaps upright. Poke a small hole in the small flap near the top. Poke another in the big flap near the one in the small flap. Push a twist-tie through the holes and twist.

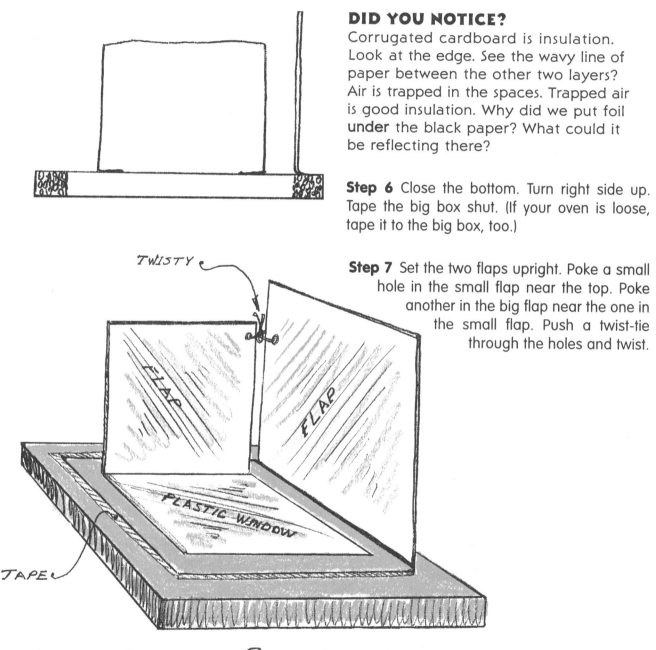

LARGE BOX WITH SMALL BOX MOUNTED INSIDE. BOTH FLAPS UP - TIED TOGETHER - WITH SHINY MATERIAL - GLUED ON - FACING IN.

# The two-flapper is ready to go!!

## Cooking with the two-flapper:

Cooking with your improved solar oven is just a little different from the first version. The flaps are fixed in place, so you don't have to adjust them. To aim it so that the most sun reflects off each flap, you point the corner **opposite** the flaps at the sun. There is a small gap between the flaps. The sun will shine through this. When that little band of sunshine lines up with the corner of the box, the aim is perfect. (If your design doesn't have this gap, use the shadow of the flaps to aim your oven.)

You might want to review the TIPS FOR USING THE PIZZA BOX SOLAR OVEN in chapter 6.

### *DO NOT LOOK AT THE SUN!!*

Before you start work in the kitchen, set the oven in the sun. This will warm things up, or preheat it, just as you would with a regular oven. It's a good idea to preheat the tray you will put the food on, too.

### *REMEMBER! USE POT HOLDERS! THAT METAL TRAY GETS HOT!!*

Don't forget to put your thermometer in the oven. (You may have to undo the twist-tie to open the oven.) Be sure to make notes about the temperature and the weather so you can compare the two-flapper to the original oven.

These recipes will not cook as fast as solar S'mores. Be patient! And keep the oven aimed at the sun.

# How to make a mini-pizza

### Ingredients

- ❏ English muffins or pita bread (toasted, if you like crusty pizza)
- ❏ pizza sauce
- ❏ shredded cheese
- ❏ topping—pepperoni, mushrooms, black olives, or . . . .(slice very thin)

## To make

Split the muffin or pita pocket in half. Spread each half with a thin layer of sauce. Sprinkle on some cheese, but not too thick. Leave some spots of sauce showing. Put on two pieces of topping. Once the cheese looks melted, the mini-pizzas are ready to eat.

**SUN FACT**

The largest pizza ever made was 122 feet, 8 inches in diameter. It was made at Norwood Hypermarket, South Africa, on December 8, 1990.

# How to make nachos

**Ingredients**

❏ corn chips

❏ shredded cheese

❏ salsa

## To make

Put a single layer of chips on the tray. Sprinkle on the cheese. Once the cheese looks melted, dip them in the salsa.

# How to make tacos

**Ingredients**

❏ tortillas (corn or flour)

❏ shredded cheese

❏ can of black beans, drained

❏ shredded lettuce

❏ salsa

## To make

Lay a tortilla on the tray. Cover one half with black beans. Cover the other half with cheese. Once the beans are warm and the cheese looks melted, the taco is cooked. Spoon on some salsa and shredded lettuce, fold over, and eat.

# Some things to think about

★ By adding another flap, we increased the amount of solar energy pouring into the oven by one-third. Did the temperature go one-third higher? For example, if the original oven hit 100°F, we would expect the two-flapper to reach about 133°F (⅓ of 100 + 100). If this didn't happen with your oven, why not? Remember, nothing is perfect! Was the weather the same? The outdoor temperature too? How about the wind?

☆ Did the two-flapper get even hotter than expected? Could the insulation have something to do with that?

✳ Did the window fog up? What's happening?

✳ Would it be a good idea if the flaps were adjustable? Take off the twist-tie and move them around. Is there an angle, other than straight up, that seems to reflect more sun into the oven? If so, can you think of an improvement to make adjustable flaps?

★ Of course, if the flaps aren't straight up, there's a big gap between them. Any way to catch that sunshine?

☆ What if you wanted to cook something in pots—like a stew, or some rice? How would the design have to change?

✧ What if you got really ambitious and wanted to make a Five-Sun oven (reflector flaps on all four sides)? How would the design have to change?

✪ Can you predict what temperature your Five-Sun oven might reach, based on what you already know? Remember, each flap adds about one-third more heat.

✳ Do you live in a place where cooking with sunshine is practical? This solar oven might not stand up to everyday use. Could you build a serious, sturdy solar oven out of other materials you can find?

**SUN FACT**

Most solar ovens that you can buy will reach temperatures between 250° and 350°F.

# Living with the sun
## Saving trees with solar ovens

Imagine what would happen if your kitchen stove disappeared. If **everyone's** kitchen stove disappeared. And the microwave. And the outdoor gas grill.

What if everyone in your neighborhood had to find some wood to cook with, every day? How long would the trees last? How far would you have to go to find wood if you lived in the city?

It's a scary idea, isn't it?

Yet nearly two billion people around the world cook their food every day over wood fires. They often live in poor countries. Women and children have to work long hours gathering firewood. Of course, the more wood that gets burned up, the fewer trees there are in the forest.

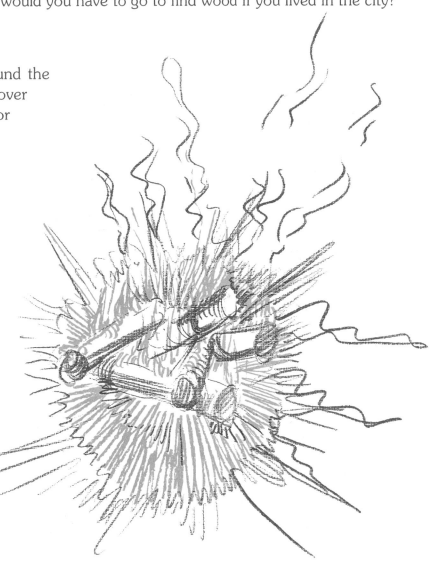

Just as in ancient Greece and Rome, many of these countries end up with an energy crisis and no trees. A world without trees isn't very pretty. It isn't healthy, either, because trees breathe in carbon dioxide and breathe out oxygen, which animals and people need to live. Trees also hold the soil in place and make shade.

You know people can cook with solar energy. You proved it with your Pizza Box Solar Oven.

It turns out that many of the countries where the forests are in danger are also countries with lots of solar energy. In places like Mexico, India, Kenya, and Peru, where the sun shines almost every day, solar cooking is practical.

Several special projects are teaching people around the world how to build their own solar ovens. One project in Arequipa, Peru, taught young people just like you how to build solar cookers. The children speak Spanish. Solar cookers are called "cocinas solares" in their language.

Guess what they used to build their cookers? Cardboard boxes and tinfoil! And for insulation, they used crumpled-up newspaper. Seems they had a solar junk box, too!

To find out what's going on with "cocinas solares" around the world, get in touch with this group:

Solar Cookers International
1724 11th Street
Sacramento, CA 95814
U.S.A.
(916) 444-6616

## SUN FACT

A poor family can spend one day each week gathering firewood just to cook their food. If they do not have wood, they use kerosene fuel, which is very expensive. Half of all the money the family earns may be spent just on kerosene!

## SUN FACT

Tom Burns used to run a restaurant. Now he designs and builds huge, portable solar ovens called "The Villager." Each oven weighs 700 pounds and sits on a trailer. They travel from village to village in poor countries. The Villager can cook 50 loaves of bread at once. Ten minutes after it is aimed at the sun, the temperature inside will reach 400°F.

# 10
# ELECTRICITY FROM SUNSHINE

## HAVE YOU EVER...?

...used solar electricity? You probably have and didn't even know it. Many pocket calculators are solar-powered and don't need batteries. When you put them in the light, they are ready to work. The solar cell is usually a small rectangle of blue glass on the calculator.

# Solar cells

Most solar cells are made of purified silicon, an element found in sand. The silicon is melted in a furnace, and a ribbon of "seed crystals" is added to the molten silicon. (If you've ever made rock candy by putting a string in a glass of super-sugary water, you can guess what happens next . . . .)

As more and more silicon crystals "grow" around the seed crystal, the furnace fills with a thick rod of silicon, called an **ingot**. After the ingot is removed from the furnace and very slowly cooled, it is sliced into thin wafers. Special coatings are added, along with a metal foil back. Wires are attached to the top and bottom. When sunlight shines on a solar cell, it generates electricity.

# Why do solar cells work?

Solar cells work because the energy in light knocks electrons off the silicon atoms in the solar cell. This is called the **photovoltaic effect**, discovered by French physicist Edmund Becquerel in 1839.

**SUN FACT**

The silicon in one ton of sand, made into solar cells, would deliver as much energy as 500,000 tons of coal.

**SUN FACT**

A solar-powered clothes dryer is very simple to make. Just string a rope between two trees and buy some clothespins!

94

The discovery that silicon makes the best solar cells was an accident. In 1954, scientists at the Bell Telephone Laboratories were experimenting with silicon for use in electronic devices like computer chips. They happened to shine a light on their bit of silicon and the needle on their power meter jumped. The silicon solar cell was born.

## SUN FACT

Solar flares are geysers of sunlight that erupt from the surface of the sun. There is enough energy in one solar flare to power all our cars, machines, houses, and factories for one billion years!

## SUN FACT

The first satellite to orbit the sun, Pioneer V, used 4,800 solar cells for power. It was launched March 11, 1960, and circled the sun between Earth and Venus.

# Solar cells in space

Since the beginning of the space program, solar cells have powered satellites and spaceships. The sun never sets in space, so solar cells work twenty-four hours a day.

Skylab was America's first space station. It had four huge solar panels to supply electricity for the astronauts living inside the space station. Special equipment let them look directly at the sun. One astronaut said the surface looked like "a great big bowl of oatmeal with pepper on it."

## Down to Earth

On Earth, solar cells supply electricity to warning buoys in the ocean, to weather stations on mountain tops, and to houses on islands. In remote African villages, they run refrigerators to keep medicines from spoiling. In India, solar cells are pumping water. Solar cells are useful wherever power lines do not go.

### HAVE YOU EVER . . . ?

. . . imagined life without electricity? No lights, TVs, computers, or video games? Half the people in the world don't have electricity in their homes.

People all over the world are discovering solar power. All that's needed are some solar panels and batteries. It only takes a few days to put a solar electric system on your house! Solar power can go wherever people go. Most solar panels are about one foot by three feet wide and weigh about the same as a gallon of milk.

# SUN FUN

## Roof watts

Here's a solar-powered calculation for you. Find out the area of your school's roof. You will need to know how long the building is and how wide it is in feet. Multiply these two numbers together. That gives you the area in square feet. Each square foot of solar panel can create about 10 watts of electricity. If you multiply the area of the roof by 10 watts, then divide by two, you will have a rough estimate of how much solar electricity your school could make when the sun is shining. (You divide by two because the solar panels have to be far enough apart not to shade each other—so some space can't be used to produce electricity.)

## SUN FACT

Bicycles are already solar-powered.
Do you know why?

## Sunshine in the tank

Solar cars make no pollution. They are quiet. Imagine what city streets would be like if all the buses and trucks and cars were solar-powered!

Many states are experimenting with electric vehicle charging stations. Instead of putting solar cells on the electric cars, engineers put them on the charging stations at commuter parking lots or on the roofs of shopping malls. The driver just plugs the car into the parking meter and drops in a few coins. Clean solar energy gets zapped into the batteries while the driver is at work or shopping!

## FRYOLATOR POWER

Solar electric cars are not the only way to go. Cars and trucks with diesel engines can run on used oil from cooking french fries. Tank getting low? Just drive in to your favorite fast food place, tell them to hold the fries and pour in the oil! Over 500,000 gallons of fryolator oil are used every year. It's made from plant seeds. And it's renewable!!

## SUN FACT

What should every solar house have? A solar robot lawnmower! These really exist and look like turtles with solar cell shells. Whenever the sun shines, the robot roams around the lawn nibbling the grass with tiny cutters.

## SUN FACT

You're not likely to see one of those fancy, high-tech solar robot lawnmowers. But keep an eye out for a low-tech, solar-powered lawnmower—that is, a goat, sheep, or cow!!

# A day at the solar races

All over the United States, kids have been designing, building, and racing their own solar electric car models for several years. These races are part of the Junior Solar Sprint project sponsored by the U.S. Department of Energy. Every racer gets exactly the same kind of solar panel and motor, but everything else about the car is up to them. The point is to build the fastest, snazziest-looking solar racer on two, three, or four wheels.

Often, science classes in one school will hold a Junior Sprint race for several nearby schools. Just like real races on a dragstrip in elimination rounds, the winners move up until a champion is found. If you would like to find out more about having a solar race in your school or town, contact the
National Renewable Energy Laboratory
1617 Cole Boulevard
Golden, CO 80401
(303) 231-1000.

**SUN FACT**

A new kind of solar cell is not fragile. Made on a flexible sheet of plastic or metal, it comes in huge rolls and can be molded to the shapes of things, like car bodies and buildings. Soon, these solar cells will take the place of regular roofs on houses. They're called "solar shingles."

# Big solar power plants

Solar cells are not the only way to make electricity with solar energy. A solar power plant in the California desert uses burning mirrors set up in long rows. The special curved mirrors reflect sunlight onto black pipes filled with water. The pipes get hot and turn the water into steam. Hundreds of mirrors must be used to make enough steam for the power plant.

The steam runs a turbine generator that makes electricity. This solar power plant makes enough electricity for 500,000 homes.

**SUN FACT**

The swimming stadium for the 1996 Summer Olympics in Atlanta, Georgia, had a solar electric power plant on its roof. The solar panels generated 340,000 watts of solar electricity.

# A pocket power plant for you

### DO YOU . . . ?

. . . use toys that need batteries?
. . . have a portable radio or cassette deck?
. . . like to go overnight camping?
. . . read by flashlight after "lights out"?

Then you could use a solar battery charger. These devices have a solar panel and a compartment for batteries. Rechargeable batteries are placed in the charger. After two or three days in the sun, they're ready to use. When the batteries run down, just pop them back in the charger! The Real Goods Trading Company sells solar battery chargers and many other fun things. Call them for a catalog at (800) 762-7325.

**SUN FACT**

Americans throw away over two billion batteries every year. Batteries poison the Earth. Let's use rechargeables!

# SUN FUN

## Become a solar engineer

Make a list of all your things that use batteries—like tape recorders, flashlights, and toys. Circle the ones you think could have solar cells on them instead of batteries—just like a solar calculator. What would your things look like with solar cells for power?

Now you are a solar engineer!

Which of your things would you like to use at night? Can you think of a way to use solar energy for them, even in the dark?

Why not take some of your snazzy designs and make them work with real solar cells? To find real solar cells, motors, gears, and other stuff, contact the Edmund Scientific Company to ask for a catalog. Call (609) 573-6260, or write them at 101 E. Gloucester Pike, Barrington, NJ 08007-1380.

HAPPY TINKERING!

# About the Author

Michael J. Daley's home in Westminster West, Vermont, is powered by solar electricity and partially heated by a greenhouse. He and his wife, author Jessie Haas, built the house themselves, including the solar systems. Michael wrote this book on a solar-powered laptop computer!

A lifelong love of energy, machines, and tinkering has led him to build models of solar ovens, wind-powered sawmills, solar cars, solar water heaters, and a working solar house model.

# About the Illustrator

As a young man, Buckley Smith sailed from his native California halfway around the world on a boat he built himself, making a living selling his art. He now lives on an offshore island in Maine where he produces work for his own gallery. With his wife and two sons, he has built two homes which are powered entirely by the sun. This is his third book.